T0358449

ROUTLEDGE LIBRARY EDITIONS:
BUSINESS AND ECONOMICS IN ASIA

Volume 10

# ECONOMIC DEVELOPMENT PATTERNS, INFLATIONS, AND DISTRIBUTIONS

# ECONOMIC DEVELOPMENT PATTERNS, INFLATIONS, AND DISTRIBUTIONS

## With Application to Korea (ROK) and Taiwan (ROC)

BYUNG OK LIM

LONDON AND NEW YORK

First published in 1991 by Garland Publishing, Inc.

This edition first published in 2019
by Routledge
2 Park Square, Milton Park, Abingdon, Oxon OX14 4RN

and by Routledge
52 Vanderbilt Avenue, New York, NY 10017

*Routledge is an imprint of the Taylor & Francis Group, an informa business*

© 1986 Byung Ok Lim

All rights reserved. No part of this book may be reprinted or reproduced or utilised in any form or by any electronic, mechanical, or other means, now known or hereafter invented, including photocopying and recording, or in any information storage or retrieval system, without permission in writing from the publishers.

*Trademark notice*: Product or corporate names may be trademarks or registered trademarks, and are used only for identification and explanation without intent to infringe.

*British Library Cataloguing in Publication Data*
A catalogue record for this book is available from the British Library

ISBN: 978-1-138-48274-6 (Set)
ISBN: 978-0-429-42825-8 (Set) (ebk)
ISBN: 978-1-138-36955-9 (Volume 10) (hbk)
ISBN: 978-0-429-42854-8 (Volume 10) (ebk)

**Publisher's Note**
The publisher has gone to great lengths to ensure the quality of this reprint but points out that some imperfections in the original copies may be apparent.

**Disclaimer**
The publisher has made every effort to trace copyright holders and would welcome correspondence from those they have been unable to trace.

# ECONOMIC DEVELOPMENT PATTERNS, INFLATIONS, AND DISTRIBUTIONS: WITH APPLICATION TO KOREA(ROK) AND TAIWAN(ROC)

by

Byung Ok Lim

Copyright © Byung Ok Lim 1986

All Rights Reserved

ABSTRACT

In the 1960s and the early 1970s, it was argued in economic literature that the drastic economic growth in the less developed countries (LDCs) brought about high rates of inflation and economic concentration.

Notably, some economists in the 1950s proposed the implicitly pessimistic inverse U-shaped hypothesis that growth and equality are mutually incompatible in the course of economic development.

According to worldwide statistics, the economic growth in the LDCs was accompanied by a worsening of the distribution of income, along with significant inflation. Most LDCs generally supported this hyposthesis of a trade-off between growth and equality.

However, in the late 1970s and the early 1980s, some economists became seriously concerned about the question of whether development strategy could manage to achieve a more equitable distribution of income, along with a moderate inflation from the benefits of economic growth. By this time, this question became the heart of one of the most debated issues in economic development.

In this matter, Korea and Taiwan contrast significantly. Korea and Taiwan are often regarded as models of successful industrialization over the last two decades. Taiwan's economy has grown rapidly and at the same time has managed to improve its distribution of income, along with a fairly stable price level. Korea also improved its distribution

TABLE OF CONTENTS

LIST OF TABLES

| Table | | Page |
|---|---|---|

| Table | | Page |
|---|---|---|

## LIST OF FIGURES

## ACKNOWLEDGMENTS

Several people have given great assistance to me in the preparation of this dissertation. Foremost among these people has been Professor Allen M. Sievers, who not only provided excellent technical assistance, but also gave much encouragement. As chairman of my supervisory committee, he has been instrumental in my completing this dissertation. Professors Stephen E. Reynolds and Lance Girton have also aided me by offering many valuable comments and by giving of their time in order to ensure that this work meets the standards of excellence established by the University of Utah.

I wish to express my gratitude to these three members of my committee for their time, patience, and expertise in assisting me. In addition to their help, however, I was initially assisted by Dr. Francis R. Lad for whom I am equally grateful.

I also wish to thank Walter Jones for his editorial assistance, and last, but not least, I wish to thank my wife, Lee, for her help and support in this endeavor.

# CHAPTER I

# INTRODUCTION

Korea's economy of the immediate postwar period was characterized by extreme economic disorganization and stagnation. These conditions were caused by sudden separation from the Japanese economy and the partition of the country along the 38th parallel. During the Japanese colonial period, the Korean economy had been highly dependent upon Japan for manpower, capital, technology, and management. The sudden separation of Korea's economy from Japan's economic control thus led to a suspension of many of Korea's economic activities. The partition also caused Korea's economy to deteriorate in terms of natural resources. Most metals, electric power, chemical products, and coal were produced in the North, while light machinery, textiles, and food were produced in the South. Thus, South Korea's economy sharply declined in every major sector because the nation was short of natural resources, skilled manpower, technology, and management.

To make the situation worse, the Korean War (1950-1953) devastated the infant industrial economy of the country and brought about the destruction of industrial plants and equipment, public utilities, private dwellings, and transportation facilities, along with the death or injury to 1.5 million civilians.

After the Korean War, roughly by 1960, Korea started to

reconstruct its war-torn economy with foreign grant aids from the United Nations Korean Reconstruction Agency (UNKRA) and the United States bilateral assistance program.

In May 1961, a military revolution overthrew the civilian government in the vortex of political and social instability. The new government, however, was anxious to revitalize the economy and set up a series of vigorous five-year economic development plans with an emphasis on leading sectors such as power plants, key manufacturing industries, primary agricultural industries, and social-overhead capital in order to stimulate economic growth.

Korea, however, has historically had a relative abundance of labor in the agricultural sector, as compared to capital. Therefore, the new government has become increasingly concerned about capital accumulation through foreign capital loans, domestic capital mobilization, and inflationary finance. In order to meet various economic development plans, the government has strongly encouraged the import of foreign capital since U.S. grant aid was drastically reduced after 1960. Thus, a foreign-capital inducement law was promulgated in January 1961 and two supplements of the law were enacted in July 1962. This law strongly stimulated the import of foreign commercial loans and foreign direct investments as one of its major policies. Tax concessions were granted to encourage foreign capital inflows and technological imports by full or partial exemptions from foreign individual and corporation income tax on foreign investments. Direct investment was much encouraged by full exemption of both income and property tax for the first five years, along with full exemption from customs duties on the imported capital goods for the approved foreign investment projects.

For domestic capital mobilization, the government passed an interest rate reform bill in September 1965. Under this financial reform, the nominal interest rate applied to one-year savings and time deposits was drastically raised to 30% in 1966 and then gradually lowered to approximately 15% by 1979. Since the financial reform was passed, the ratio of gross domestic savings to GNP has tremendously increased from less than 4% in the early 1960s to 16% in 1970 and 28% in 1979, a savings record in the history of Korea. Most of these savings, however, were generated from the business and government sectors rather than from the general public's own savings. During this study period, the entire banking system in Korea was completely controlled by the government. Thus, foreign, government, business, and private household savings were allocated by the government and channeled to preferred exporting industries.

In addition to foreign and domestic savings, the government had access to extra resources from inflationary monetary expansion based on revenue from a seigniorage-cum-inflation tax in order to finance various industrial development plans. This revenue from inflationary monetary expansion was also subsidized to preferred exporting industries at low interest rates through the central bank rediscount process. Thus, the government discriminately subsidized massive credits of financial resources in monetary form to the industrial sector at preferential interest rates. These financial resources from foreign savings, domestic savings, and new-money creation have transferred to preferred industries and selected entrepreneurs. This has resulted in a tremendous accumulation of capital and technological improvements in the nonagricultural sector.

Faced as it was with surplus labor in the agricultural sector, the basic challenge to Korea's economy was how to transfer the redundant agricultural labor force to nonagricultural activities. This redundant labor force was unable to make a productive contribution to agricultural output. Therefore, it was believed that reallocating the surplus portions of the labor force to the non-agricultural sector would make a positive contribution to total national output. This reallocation and its concomitant utilization in the nonagricultural sector constituted the central point of the economic development problem during President Park's administration.

In this context, the development-oriented policy of the government attempted to remove the rural surplus labor force via channeling the subsidized financial resources to the exporting industries. Thus, a rapid capital accumulation with new foreign technology absorbed a significant portion of the labor force from the agricultural sector. Consequently, the economic center of gravity graudally shifted from agricultural to nonagricultural activities in the course of industrialization during the last two decades. Particularly, the capital-intensive industrialization changed the structure of the economy to form new patterns of production technique, productivity, employment, wage structure, national income, and income distribution.

Thus, the rapid growth in economic factors (capital, labor, and technology) between the rural and modern sectors clearly affected a remarkable increase in national income (9.8% per annum during the period 1961-1979) and also influenced the distribution of income in Korea's dualistic economy.

Intersectorally, the relative share of the agricultural income continually decreased as the economic activities shifted from the agricultural to the nonagricultural sector. In the nonagricultural sector, however, the share of the income persistently increased in the course of resources reallocation.

Within the nonagricultural sector, the distributive share of wage income generally decreased in spite of a drastic increase in wage rates after the economic turning point. Accordingly, the share of property income significantly increased in the functional distribution process in the same period.

In size distribution of income, the overall household's distirbution of income displayed a considerable tendency toward improvement from 1965 to 1970 in the course of rapid economic growth and then demonstrated a significant downward trend in the 1970s. Thus, Korea's rapid economic growth experienced a particular pattern of income distribution (a U-shaped pattern), rather than the inverse U-shaped pattern which usually takes place in the less developed countries.

In addition, the income gaps between the agricultural and nonagricultural sectors, between the workers and capital-entrepreneurs, and even between the unprivileged and privileged entrepreneurs significantly diverged in the course of industrialization since 1970. This situation is considered to be not only an economic problem, but also a pending sociopolitical issue as a by-product of economic growth.

## The Purpose of This Study

This study will examine the growth process of Korea's dualistic economy, the sectoral, functional, and size distributions, and the causal relationship between growth and distribution. Thus, the distribution of income will be analyzed in relation to changes in economic factors and to economic growth in Korea's particular development process.

Consequently, this paper will survey the dualistic economic growth in Korea in terms of economic factor growth (capital, labor, and technology). In turn, the changing distribution of income will be traced to the dualistic economic growth which occurred in the course of industrialization.

The sectoral distribution is to be investigated in terms of the economic center of gravity which shifted from the agricultural to the nonagricultural sector. The functional distribution is also to be examined in relation to changes in capital, labor, and technology in the nonagricultural sector. These two growth-relevant distributions, along with the distorted financial system, will be analyzed in terms of quantifying their effects on the overall household distribution of income.

Basically, the inequality of the overall distribution of income is to be broken down into the three deterministic factor components; (1) the reallocation effect (sectoral distribution effect),

(2) the functional distribution effect, and (3) the factor Gini effect.

The main interests in this study are focused on these issues as follows:

1. In an attempt to achieve a "quick big-push" regarding industrial economic growth, capital was improperly increased relative to labor through a policy of massive capital mobilization in the industrial sector, leaving the agricultural sector lagging. Such an unbalanced growth path not only led to a serious intersectoral income disparity, but also had significant impact on the overall distribution of income.
2. Korea's unbalanced growth pattern has not been conducive to achieving efficient utilization of resources, and has thus reduced potential national income in the development process.
3. This unbalanced growth path (the improperly capital-intensive industrialization combined with inadequate agricultural participation) experienced an earlier advent of cost-push inflation pressure than usual. Consequently, following the economic turning point, there was a spiral acceleration of capital formation within the nonagricultural sector.
4. The immoderate capital-deepening industrialization, as a result of the early advent of the economic turning point around 1966, inevitably brought about a labor-saving direction in technological progress after 1970. This had a significant impact on a decrease in the labor share and also on an

increase in the inequality of the overall distribution of income.

5. The relative share of agricultural income in national income gradually decreased in the course of the resource reallocation from the agricultural to the nonagricultural sector. Accordingly, the share of nonagricultural income increased as the economic center of gravity shifted from the agricultural to the nonagricultural activity. This resource reallocation effect had an adverse impact on the overall household distribution of income.
6. In the nonagricultural sector, the technological progress was biased in a labor-using direction from 1965 to 1970 and then switched to a labor-saving direction in the 1970s. Therefore, the labor-using technological progress had a favorable effect on the labor share in the functional distribution for the period of 1965-1970 and the labor-saving technological progress had an adverse effect on the labor share in the 1970s.
7. However, both factor-biased technological progresses (labor-using technological progress before 1970 and labor-saving technological progress after 1970) in the nonagricultural sector had an unfavorable effect on the overall distribution of income before and after 1970, respectively.
8. The nonagricultural income improved significantly so that the highly favorable nonagricultural Gini effect overwhelmed all the growth-relevant effects. Therefore, the net effect,

as a whole, resulted in the favorable change in the overall distribution of income. Consequently, Korea experienced "Growth with Equality" in the course of industrialization before 1970.

9. The distorted financial system after 1970 had a significant adverse effect on the overall distribution of income, particularly on the nonagricultural income distribution. This effect increased the inequality of the overall distribution of income from .332 in 1970 to .381 in 1976.
10. Thus, Korea's economic growth experienced a particular distribution pattern, namely, a "U-shaped pattern" of the distribution of income in the growth path, while Taiwan's balanced growth path led to a "straight downward pattern" of improvement in the distribution of income during the past two decades.
11. The experiences of Korea and Taiwan indicate that there is nothing inevitable about the appearance of a Kuznets-Myrdal's effect in the course of rapid economic growth in the LDCs.
12. Generally, this paper hypothesizes that the unbalanced growth path would experience, not only an inflationary growth, but also a worsening of the distribution of income in the developing countries.

# CHAPTER II

## FACTOR GROWTH

The major, well-recognized economic problem of the developing economy is the existence of over-population in the agricultural sector and the shortage of capital in the nonagricultural sector. Korea has not been an exception in this respect. The distinctive feature of Korea's labor-surplus economy was the predominance of an agricultural sector characterized by widespread disguised under-employment and high rates of population growth in the 1950s and in the early 1960s.

For this type of economy, it is possible to view the essential production conditions in the agricultural sector as the existence of a redundant agricultural labor force, the fixity of land, and the operation of the law of diminishing returns to labor.

In contrast to the agricultural sector, the primary problem in the industrial sector in Korea has been the shortage of capital, skilled labor, and technology. It was, therefore, recognized that the process of industrialization necessitated the accumulation of physical capital as a prerequisite to absorbing the surplus labor force.

The existence of a surplus agricultural labor force was a highly significant phenomenon in view of the fact that a portion of the labor force was unable to make a productive contribution to agricultural output. Thus, the major problem of Korea's economy was the reallocation of the redundant portions of the labor force to alternative employment where it would be able to make a positive contribution to total national output.

In this context, the development-oriented policy of the government attempted to absorb the redundant rural labor force via channeling the financial resources of domestic savings, foreign savings, and even monetary expansion to fuel industrial expansion.

## Savings and Capital Accumulation

Government policy strongly enhanced the mobilization of capital through domestic and foreign savings. These savings were channeled to investment funds for industrial development and contributed to a dramatic change in capital formation in the nonagricultural sector during the 1960s and 1970s.

In order to achieve the goal of capital mobilization, the government attempted various economic reforms, of which the interest-rate reform of September 1965 had a tremendous impact, not only on domestic savings, but also on foreign capital inflows. This reform substantially raised the interest rate on savings deposits from 15% (applied to time deposits for one year) to 30% and created a large interest rate differential in order to stimulate voluntary private savings while simultaneously reallocating investment funds to their most effective use. Thus, this effort made possible a significantly higher ratio of investment to national income.

Domestic savings are derived from two main sources: government savings and private savings (business and household). In the early 1960s (1961-1963), the government sector shows dissavings (deficit budgets). After 1964 (the tax-reform of 1964), however, governmental budgetary surpluses were continually created due to the rapid growth in tax revenues, increases in profits from government-run monopoly enterprises, and a slow rate of increase in current government expenditures. Thus, government savings continually increased and the ratio of government savings to the GNP remained below 7% throughout the 15 years from 1964 to 1979 (see Table 1).

These government savings were mostly reinvested in government-run enterprises such as electric power, transportation, communication, and other forms of social overhead. The remainder was then channeled to the private industrial sector through the government-financed loan funds of the development banking institutions (The Korean Development Bank and the Medium Industry Bank).

On the other hand, the private savings ratio showed marked improvement from the low level of the period 1961-1965 when it remained below 7% of the GNP. Rapid acceleration occurred after the interest rate reform of September 1965. In 1966, the ratio jumped to 9% and then fluctuated between 7.4% and 9.5% until 1971. Thereafter, the savings ratio drastically increased from 8.5% in 1971 to 12.7% in 1975, to 15.2% in 1976, and to 21.5% in 1979. Thus, private savings, after the interest-rate reform, made a major contribution to the increase in total domestic savings.

It generally appears that the two reforms (tax and interest rate) played an important role in increasing total domestic savings.

TABLE 1

COMPOSTION OF DOMESTIC SAVINGS AND SAVINGS RATIO, 1961-1979
(Unit: In billion won)

| (1) | (2) | | (3) | | (4) | | (5) |
|---|---|---|---|---|---|---|---|
| Year | Government Savings (% of GNP) | | Private Savings (% of GNP) | | Total Domestic Savings (% of GNP) | | GNP |
| 1961 | -5.30 | (-1.8) | 16.88 | (5.7) | 11.58 | (3.9) | 297.08 |
| 1963 | -1.32 | (-0.3) | 31.81 | (6.5) | 30.49 | (6.2) | 488.54 |
| 1964 | 3.55 | (0.5) | 48.39 | (6.9) | 51.94 | (7.4) | 700.20 |
| 1965 | 14.02 | (1.7) | 46.48 | (5.8) | 60.59 | (7.5) | 805.32 |
| 1966 | 19.08 | (1.8) | 93.37 | (9.0) | 112.45 | (10.9) | 1,032.45 |
| 1968 | 100.61 | (6.3) | 117.71 | (7.4) | 218.32 | (13.7) | 1,598.04 |
| 1970 | 180.00 | (7.0) | 245.20 | (9.5) | 425.20 | (16.4) | 2,589.26 |
| 1971 | 190.10 | (6.0) | 268.17 | (8.5) | 458.27 | (14.5) | 3,151.55 |
| 1975 | 479.19 | (5.3) | 1,156.70 | (12.7) | 1,635.89 | (18.0) | 9,080.33 |
| 1976 | 600.99 | (4.6) | 1,988.05 | (15.2) | 2,589.04 | (19.8) | 13,051.25 |
| 1979 | 1,950.46 | (6.6) | 6,355.05 | (21.5) | 8,305.51 | (28.1) | 29,553.68 |

SOURCE: The Bank of Korea, Economic Statistics Yearbook (Seoul, 1977) and The Bank of Korea, Monthly Economic Statistics (Seoul, January 1980), p. 140.

In the early 1960s (1961-1965), the total domestic savings ratio of GNP stayed below 7.5%. However, after the two reforms, the total domestic savings ratio drastically rose from 7.5% in 1965 to 10.9% in 1966, to 18.0% in 1975, and to 28.1% in 1979. This became a savings record for Korea.

In addition to the domestic savings mobilization, foreign savings inflow significantly contributed to the national investment needs in the industrial sector. This inflow eased Korea's development path and accelerated its pace of economic growth.

The government became increasingly concerned about a loan type of foreign capital inducement to finance the various development plans in the industrial sector since the U.S. grant-aids were continually reduced after 1961. Accordingly, a foreign-capital inducement law was promulgated in January 1961 and two supplements of the law were enacted in July 1962.

According to the law, tax concessions were granted to attract both foreign capital and technology by full or partial exemption from individual and corporation income tax on all foreign investment. These concessions included an exemption from the customs duties on imported capital goods for approved foreign investment projects.

Furthermore, the interest-rate reform of 1965, which raised capital prices, and the real-wage stabilization policy substantially stimulated the foreign savings inflows for investment in Korea's industrial sector.

Table 2 shows that the foreign savings (transfer and loans)

TABLE 2

DOMESTIC, FOREIGN SAVINGS AND GROSS DOMESTIC CAPITAL FORMATION, 1961-1979
(Unit: In billion won)

| (1) Year | (2) Domestic Savings (% of GNP) | (3) Foreign Savings (Transfer & Loans) (% of GNP) | (4) Gross Domestic Capital Formation (% of GNP) | (5) Gross Domestic Fixed Capital Formation |
|---|---|---|---|---|
| 1961 | 11.58 (3.9) | 25.29 (8.5) | 38.79 (13.1) | 34.29 |
| 1962 | 5.48 (1.6) | 37.95 (10.9) | 45.47 (13.0) | 48.62 |
| 1963 | 30.49 (6.2) | 52.36 (10.7) | 90.26 (18.5) | 68.04 |
| 1964 | 51.94 (7.4) | 49.13 (7.0) | 102.24 (14.6) | 81.44 |
| 1965 | 60.50 (7.5) | 51.53 (6.4) | 121.98 (15.1) | 119.17 |
| 1966 | 112.45 (10.9) | 87.63 (8.5) | 224.48 (21.7) | 208.69 |
| 1967 | 151.81 (12.0) | 112.86 (10.9) | 280.97 (27.2) | 272.96 |
| 1968 | 218.32 (13.7) | 184.33 (11.5) | 427.87 (26.8) | 411.66 |
| 1969 | 365.18 (17.5) | 229.02 (11.0) | 620.70 (29.8) | 552.94 |
| 1970 | 425.20 (16.4) | 249.31 (9.6) | 704.66 (27.2) | 650.20 |
| 1971 | 458.27 (14.5) | 354.00 (11.2) | 805.35 (25.6) | 729.72 |
| 1972 | 577.37 (15.0) | 215.03 (5.6) | 805.48 (20.9) | 780.23 |
| 1973 | 1,083.57 (22.1) | 198.92 (4.1) | 1,288.89 (26.3) | 1,169.43 |
| 1974 | 1,302.19 (19.3) | 901.79 (13.5) | 2,102.06 (31.2) | 1,754.95 |
| 1975 | 1,635.89 (18.0) | 1,022.99 (11.3) | 2,478.39 (27.3) | 2,331.85 |
| 1976 | 2,589.04 (19.8) | 320.51 (2.5) | 3,371.71 (25.8) | 3,152.37 |
| 1977 | 4,278.32 (25.0) | 101.93 (0.6) | 4,644.95 (27.1) | 4,420.88 |
| 1978 | 6,044.35 (26.4) | 753.54 (3.3) | 7,137.74 (31.1) | 7,023.07 |
| 1979 | 8,305.51 (28.1) | 1,926.17 (6.5) | 10,596.69 (35.9) | 9,344.14 |

SOURCE: The Bank of Korea, Economic Statistics Yearbook (Seoul, 1977), p.296; The Bank of Korea, Monthly Economic Statistics (Seoul, January 1980), p. 140.

NOTE: Column (5) = Gross Domestic Capital Formation - Inventory Stock.

contributed the major component of gross capital formation, averaging 10% of the GNP over the three years from 1961 to 1963. Over the same period, however, domestic savings became the minor component of gross capital formation, averaging 3.9% of the GNP. Thus, foreign savings accounted for 66% of capital formation and domestic savings accounted for 27%, as shown in Table 3.

After 1963, foreign savings significantly declined relative to domestic savings as a source of capital formation. From 1964 through 1975, foreign savings averaged 9.2% of the GNP, contributing the minor component of gross capital formation. Thus, foreign savings accounted for 37% of gross capital formation and domestic savings accounted for 65% (Table 3).

During 1976-1979, foreign savings further dropped to an annual average of 3.2% of the GNP and thus, accounted for 12% of gross capital formation. Meanwhile, domestic savings accounted for 82% of capital formation, averaging 24.8% of the GNP during the same period. Thus, domestic savings financed most of Korea's domestic investment needs.

It appears that rapidly increasing domestic savings and the steady inflow of foreign savings enabled Korea to achieve a high rate of gross domestic capital formation from 1961 to 1979. Consequently, the domestic capital formation, as shown in Table 2, column 4, grew at a remarkable annual rate of 37% from 1961 to 1979.

## Fixed Capital Stock

This paper is interested in tracing Korea's domestic capital formation to its fixed capital stock in the economy as a whole and in

TABLE 3

COMPOSITION OF GROSS CAPITAL FORMATION, 1961-1979
(Percent)

| (1) Year | (2) Share of Domestic Savings | (3) Share of Foreign Savings | (4) Statistical Error |
|---|---|---|---|
| 1961-1963 | 27 | 66 | -7 |
| 1964-1975 | 65 | 37 | +2 |
| 1976-1979 | 82 | 12 | -6 |

SOURCE: Table 2.

the nonagricultural sector specifically.

For calculation of fixed capital stock, Professor K. C. Han[1] estimated the total fixed capital stock of the whole economy on the basis of the National Wealth Survey of 1968.[2] The total gross fixed capital stock (undepreciated) was estimated to be 4,836.416 billion won which was then adjusted to 3,163.500 billion won as the net fixed capital stock of 1968 (Table 4, column 3). Finally, the net fixed capital stock of 1968 was deflated by the 1970 won value to 3,970.161 billion won which is the real net fixed capital stock of 1968 as a benchmark (Table 4, column 4).

The annual net fixed capital stocks for years other than the benchmark year of 1968 may be calculated from the capital stock of the benchmark year as folows:

$$K_t = K^*_{t-1} + \Delta K_t - D_t \qquad (1)$$

where $K^*_{t-1}$ : net fixed capital stock at constant price in t - 1 year as a benchmark.

$\Delta K_t$ : fixed capital formation at constant price in year t.

$D_t$ : provisions for consumption of fixed capital stock at constant price in year t.

and $K_t$ : net fixed capital stock at constant price in year t.

---

[1]K. C. Han, Estimates of Korean Capital and Inventory Coefficient in 1969 (Seoul: Yonsei University Press, 1970).

[2]Economic Planning Board, Report on National Wealth Survey (as of December 1968) (Seoul, 1972).

TABLE 4

SECTORAL GROSS AND NET FIXED CAPITAL STOCK, 1968

| (1) | (2) | (3) | (4) | (5) |
|---|---|---|---|---|
| | | Han's Net Fixed Capital Stock | | |
| Industry | Han's Gross Capital Stock (Undepreciated in Million 1968 Won) | Uniform Net Adjustments [(2) x .6448] | Net Stock in Million 1970 Won | Net Stock in Million 1970 Dollars [(4)/310.6] |
| Agriculture, Forestry and Fishery | 353,896 | 228.173 | 261,967 | 843.4 |
| Mining and Quarrying | 34,747 | 22,403 | 26,295 | 84.7 |
| Manufacturing | 720,190 | 464,339 | 522,316 | 1,681.6 |
| Construction | 53,036 | 34,159 | 38,814 | 125.0 |
| Electricity, Water and Sanitary Services | 145,448 | 139,019 | 175,751 | 565.8 |
| Transporation, Storage and Communication | 730,945 | 471,273 | 580,386 | 1,868.6 |
| Wholesale and Retail Trade | 169,060 | 109,001 | 126,013 | 405.7 |
| Banking, Insurance and Real Estate | 24,955 | 16,090 | 19,132 | 61.6 |
| Public Administration | 237,716 | 153,266 | 146,228 | 599.6 |
| Services | 574,982 | 370,717 | 444,505 | 1,431.1 |
| Ownership of Dwellings | 1,791,441 | 1,155,024 | 1,588,754 | 5,115.1 |
| Total Fixed Capital Stock | 4,836,416 | 3,163,500 | 3,970,161 | 12,782.2 |

SOURCE: K. C. Han, *Estimates of Korean Capital and Inventory Coefficients in 1968*, (Seoul: Yonsei University, 1970); Economic Planning Board, *Report on National Wealth Survey* (as of December 31, 1968) (Seoul, 1972).

The result of this calculation (Table 5) shows that the respective net fixed capital stock totals for 1961, 1970, and 1979 amount to 2,732.13, 4,954.20, and 12,763.15 billion won. This capital stock increased at an average rate of 6.8% per year during the 1960s and 11.2% during the 1970s. From 1961 to 1979, the whole economy's capital stock grew at a rate of 8.9% per annum, as shown in Table 5, column 5.

For the calculation of nonagricultural capital stock, we use the same proecedure as used in Equation 1, which was based on Professor Han's net fixed capital stock estimate for 1968. Excluding agricultural capital stock and ownership of dwellings, Han's estimate of the nonagricultural net fixed capital stock of 1968 became 2,119.44 billion won as a benchmark (Table 6, column 5). This figure may be computed by subtracting both the agricultural net fixed capital stock (261.967 billion won) and the ownership of dwellings (1,588.754 billion won) from the total net fixed capital stock for 1968 (3,970.161 billion won) as shown in Table 4, column 4.

Consequently, one may compute the nonagricultural net fixed capital stock for years other than a benchmark year by subtracting (or adding) the net annual fixed capital formation of nonagricultural sector from (to) the nonagricultural net fixed capital stock for 1968 (*2,119.44 billion won). Thus, the nonagricultural sector's net annual fixed capital stock has been computed for the years 1961 to 1979, as shown in Table 6, column 5. This table shows that the respective net fixed capital stock totals for 1961, 1970, and 1979 amounted to 1,185.34 billion won, 2,897.25 billion won, and 8,263.09

TABLE 5

FIXED CAPITAL STOCK (WHOLE ECONOMY), 1961-1979
(Unit: In billion 1970 won)

| (1) Year | (2) Gross Fixed Capital Formation ($\Delta K_t$) | (3) Provisions for Consumption of Fixed Capital Formation ($D_t$) | (4) Net Fixed Capital Formation ($\Delta K_t - D_t$) | (5) Net Fixed Capital Stock ($K_t$) |
|---|---|---|---|---|
| 1961 | 104.45 | 44.20 | 60.29 | 2,732.13 |
| 1962 | 133.40 | 52.09 | 81.32 | 2,813.45 |
| 1963 | 167.79 | 65.07 | 102.72 | 2,916.17 |
| 1964 | 155.08 | 70.63 | 84.45 | 3,000.62 |
| 1965 | 195.43 | 75.41 | 120.02 | 3,120.64 |
| 1966 | 294.29 | 83.52 | 210.77 | 3,331.41 |
| 1967 | 358.65 | 98.40 | 260.25 | 3,591.66 |
| 1968 | 498.30 | 119.80 | 378.50 | *3,970.16 |
| 1969 | 639.24 | 145.30 | 493.95 | 4,464.10 |
| 1970 | 650.24 | 160.16 | 490.09 | 4,954.20 |
| 1971 | 680.59 | 178.47 | 502.12 | 5,456.32 |
| 1972 | 659.12 | 232.36 | 426.76 | 5,883.08 |
| 1973 | 851.85 | 296.13 | 555.72 | 6,438.80 |
| 1974 | 939.07 | 313.98 | 625.08 | 7,063.88 |
| 1975 | 1,060.41 | 342.10 | 718.31 | 7,782.19 |
| 1976 | 1,238.65 | 412.44 | 826.21 | 8,608.40 |
| 1977 | 1,468.73 | 459.41 | 1,009.32 | 9,617.72 |
| 1978 | 1,934.20 | 454.40 | 1,479.80 | 11,097.52 |
| 1979 | 2,136.78 | 471.15 | 1,665.63 | 12,763,15 |

SOURCE: Columns (2) and (3) are from The Bank of Korea, Economic Statistics Yearbook (Seoul, 1977), pp. 270-271 and The Bank of Korea, Monthly Economic Statistics (Seoul, January 1980), pp. 134-137.

NOTE: Column (4) is obtained by subtracting column (3) from column (2). Column (5) is calculated according to the equation $K_t = K^*_{t-1} + \Delta K_t - D_t$ on the base of the net fixed capital stock of 1968 (*3,970.16) as a benchmark.

The net fixed capital stock of 1968 is from Han's estimate in Table 4.

The implicit GNP deflator is applied to obtain the 1970 value.

TABLE 6

FIXED CAPITAL STOCK IN NONAGRICULTURAL SECTOR, 1961-1979
(Unit: In billion 1970 won)

| (1) Year | (2) Gross Fixed Capital Formation ($\Delta K_t$) | (3) Provisions for Consumption of Fixed Capital Formation ($D_t$) | (4) Net Fixed Capital Formation (2) - (3) | (5) Net Fixed Capital Stock ($K_t$) |
|---|---|---|---|---|
| 1961 | 71.18 | 33.45 | 38.33 | 1,185.34 |
| 1962 | 104.11 | 40.50 | 63.61 | 1,248.95 |
| 1963 | 129.33 | 52.68 | 76.66 | 1,325.61 |
| 1964 | 112.00 | 56.19 | 55.81 | 1,381.42 |
| 1965 | 145.14 | 61.65 | 83.49 | 1,464.91 |
| 1966 | 223.66 | 69.02 | 154.65 | 1,619.56 |
| 1967 | 285.10 | 80.76 | 204.34 | 1,823.91 |
| 1968 | 396.02 | 100.48 | 295.54 | *2,119.44 |
| 1969 | 527.86 | 122.87 | 404.99 | 2,524.43 |
| 1970 | 509.94 | 137.13 | 372.81 | 2,897.25 |
| 1971 | 528.73 | 151.54 | 377.19 | 3,274.44 |
| 1972 | 497.71 | 202.23 | 295.47 | 3,559.91 |
| 1973 | 655.80 | 261.46 | 394.34 | 3,964.25 |
| 1974 | 669.44 | 281.63 | 387.75 | 4,352.00 |
| 1975 | 774.40 | 303.65 | 470.84 | 4,822.84 |
| 1976 | 934.06 | 370.04 | 564.02 | 5,386.86 |
| 1977 | 1,094.95 | 409.89 | 685.06 | 6,071.92 |
| 1978 | 1,402.10 | 413,35 | 988.75 | 7,060.67 |
| 1979 | 1,643.19 | 440.77 | 1,202.42 | 8,263.09 |

SOURCE: Data (columns (2) and (3)) are obtained from The Bank of Korea, *Economic Statistics Yearbook* (Seoul, 1977), pp. 268-269 and The Bank of Korea, *Monthly Economic Statistics* (Seoul, January 1980), pp. 134-137.

NOTE: Column (4) is obtained by subtracting column (3) from column (2). Column (5) is calculated according to the equation $K_t = K^*_{t-1} + \Delta K_t - D_t$ on the base of the net fixed capital stock of 1968 (*2,119.44) as a benchmark.

Agricultural net fixed capital stock and dwellings are excluded from these data.

billion won, respectively. Therefore, the nonagricultural capital stock increased at an annual average rate of 5.4% from 1961 to 1965, 14.6% from 1965 to 1970, 10.7% from 1970 to 1975, and 14.4% from 1975 to 1979. In the early 1960s, the nonagricultural sector's net fixed capital stock increased moderately, but then accelerated tremendously from the late 1960s through 1979 as a result of Korea's financial reforms. Thus, nonagricultural capital stock growth averaged 11.4% per annum from 1961 to 1979.

The government-driven high rates of capital formation, thus, contributed to a remarkable increase in capital stock in Korea's economy. This, in turn, had a significant impact on the structure of the economy, especially on labor absorption, national income, and income distribution.

## Labor Absorption and Employment

A basic policy measure of the developing dualistic economy faced with an initially unfavorable endowment and an increase in population pressure is to reallocate as much labor as possible from its agricultural sector to its nonagricultural sector. This process of labor reallocation must be sufficiently rapid to shift the economy's center of gravity from the agricultural to the nonagricultural sector.

The rapidity of labor absorption in the nonagricultural sector depends not only on the rapidity of capital accumulation but also on the strength of the technological progress in the nonagricultural sector. Here, capital accumulation and technological progress can be considered as causal agents for the labor absorption as in the following labor absorption equation:[3]

$$G_L + \frac{G_W}{E_{LL}} = G_K + \frac{B_L + T}{E_{LL}} \qquad (2)$$

where $G_x$ is the growth rate of a variable of subscript x,

so that $G_L$ : rate of growth of labor

$G_w$ : rate of wage growth

$G_k$ : rate of capital growth

and $B_L$ : labor-biased technological progress

$T$ : rate of neutral technological progress,

and $E_{LL}$: elasticity of the marginal product of labor with respect to labor.

This equation shows that the labor absorption and the change in wage rate are endogenously determined by the two exogenous forces of capital accumulation and technological change. More precisely, capital accumulation ($G_k$) and/or intensity of neutral technological progress (T) and/or labor-using bias ($B_L$) will have an impact either on the rate of labor absorption ($G_L$) or on the wage level ($G_w$) or on both of them. Thus, the effects of the exogenous forces of the right-hand side of the equation can be absorbed by the change in the amount of absorbed labor or the change in the level of real wage in the development process.

---

[3]John C. H. Fei and Gustav Ranis, Development of the Labor Surplus Economy (New Haven: The Economic Center, Yale University Press, 1964), p. 91. The authors derived the labor absorption equation from the aggregate production function in their book's appendix, pp. 101-109.

In the presence of an unlimited supply of labor, the real wage is institutionally fixed at a subsistence wage level which means that the labor absorption equation can be changed to:

$$G_L = G_K + \frac{B_L + T}{E_{LL}} \qquad (3)^4$$

$$(G_w = 0)$$

where changes in the exogenous forces of capital accumulation ($G_k$) and combined technological progress [$(B_L + T)/E_{LL}$] have an impact entirely on factor-quantity adjustment, such as labor absorption ($G_L$). The capital accumulation and the intensity of combined technological change should determine the strength of the pulling forces only for labor from the agricultural sector.

It is easier to understand the effects of capital accumulation and combined technological progress on labor absorption by visualizing the process graphically. In Figure 1, we can clearly see the labor absorption process in the course of capital accumulation and technological progress over time. For convenience's sake, we assume that the production function satisfies the conditions of the competitive situation, the constant return to scale, and the well-behaved contour. In part A, capital and labor are measured on the vertical and on the horizontal axes, respectively. The solid contour lines ($V_0$, $V_1$) represent the production isoquants before biased technological progress where $OK_0$ units of capital are being applied, together with $OL_0$ units of labor, to produce $V_0$ units of output at $P_0$. The dotted contour lines

---

[4]Ibid., p. 93.

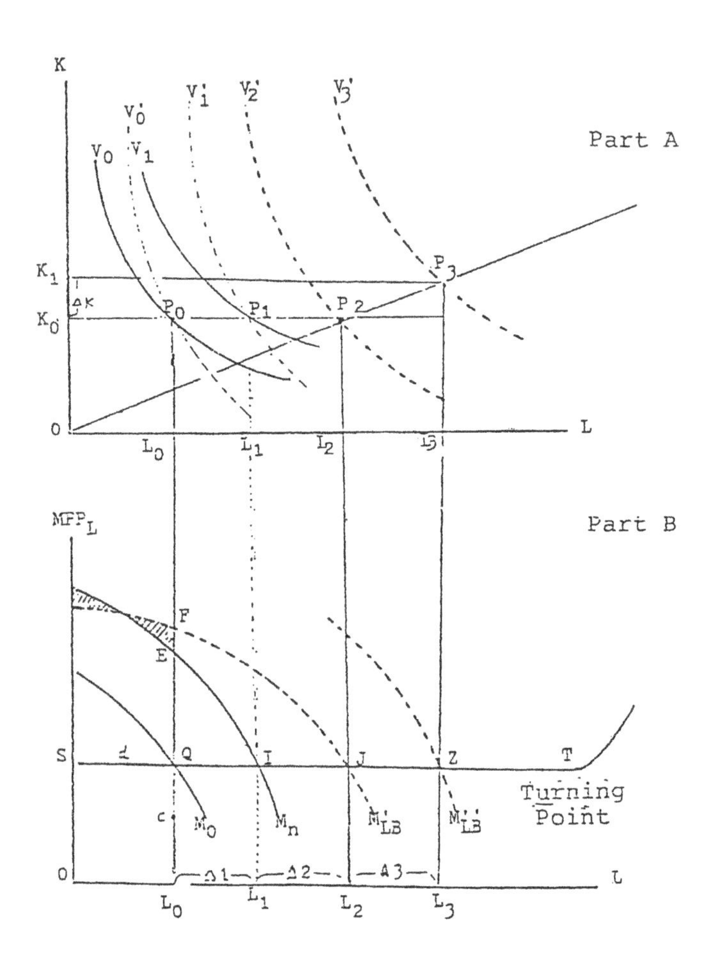


Fig. 1. Capital accumulation, technology progress, and labor absorption. Labor-biased technological progress is assumed in the figure.

($V'_0$, $V'_1$, $V'_2$, and $V'_3$) indicate the production isoquants after the labor-biased technological progress. In Part B, the marginal productivity curves (solid and dotted) on the quadrant between $MPP_L$ (marginal physical product of labor) on the vertical axis and L (labor) on the horizontal axis represent their corresponding derivatives from the production isoquants of Part A.

Now, let us see how the labor absorption process is affected by $G_k$, $B_L$, T, and $E_{LL}$. In the presence of an unlimited supply of labor ($G_w = 0$, fixed wage level: ST in Part B) the labor absorption due to neutral technological progress (T) is indicated by $\Delta 1$, which is the distance $L_0L_1$. As a result of the effect of labor-biased technological progress ($B_L$), however, additional units of labor, $\Delta 2$ ($L_1L_2$), will be absorbed by the nonagricultural sector. Furthermore, the labor absorption due only to the effect of change in capital stock from $K_0$ to $K_1$ ($G_k$) is represented by $\Delta 3$ units of labor ($L_2L_3$), which is entirely independent of the technological progress. Finally, the condition of diminishing returns ($E_{LL}$: elasticity of marginal productivity of labor with respect to labor) also has an impact on the labor absorption. This means that the less strong the magnitude of diminishing returns becomes ($MPP_L$ curves become more flat, that is $E_{LL}$ is smaller), the more the amount of labor will be absorbed.

Sooner or later, the economy will reach a point at which the unlimited supply of labor comes to an end as the center of gravity of the economy shifts toward the nonagricultural sector. The agricultural surplus labor force is gradually exhausted as the industrial labor absorption process continues through time. Once the pool of surplus labor dries up, any further reallocation will lead to increases of real wage in both sectors because labor has now become a scarce factor. As labor becomes more expensive the entrepreneur is induced to substitute capital for labor in the production techniques. Thus, when the unlimited supply of labor comes to an end, the economy approaches a so-called "turning point" (at T in Figure 1) where the real wage will be pushed up from its constancy (ST) and more capital will be substituted for labor. Consequently, at the turning point the impact of variations in the magnitude of the exogenous forces in the right hand side of Equation 2 will be absorbed either by factor-quanity adjustment or by factor-price adjustment. In other words, the exogenous forces, namely capital accumulation and combined technological progress, causally determine the rapidity of labor absorption ($G_L$) and/or the rapidity of the increase of the real wage ($G_w$).

So far, the labor absorption process from the theoretical viewpoint of Professors Fei and Ranis has been mentioned. Now, the Korean experience with labor absorption as it was affected by capital accumulation, technological progress, and changes in real wage will be illustrated.

The total change in labor absorption (dL/dt: Table 7, column 2) can be divided into the three flexible terms: wage effect, capital effect, and technological effect. During the period 1961-1965, the average change equal to 255.75 thousands of employment per annum was composed of 155.45 thousands of employment of the capital effect, 25.72 thousands of the technological effect, and 74.58 thousands of the wage effect. Here, the real wage decreased at 2.75%

TABLE 7

THE EFFECT OF CAPITAL AND TECHNOLOGY ON LABOR ASSORPTION IN THE NONAGRICULTURAL SECTOR, 1961-1979
(Unit: In thousand man-years)

| (1) Period Annual Average | (2) $\frac{dL}{dt}$ ($G_L$) | (3) Wage Growth ($G_w$) | (4) Wage Effect ($G_w/E_{LL}$) | (5) Capital Effect ($G_k$) | (6) Techno-logical Effect $(B_L+T)/E_{LL}$ |
|---|---|---|---|---|---|
| (1st) 1961-1965 | 255.75 (8.95) | (-2.75) | -74.58 (-2.61) | 155.45 (5.44) | 25.72 (.90) |
| (2nd) 1965-1970 | 243.40 (6.16) | (8.12) | 385.65 (9.76) | 578.87 (14.65) | 50.18 (1.27) |
| (3rd) 1970-1975 | 333.00 (6.25) | (3.38) | 290.38 (5.45) | 572.23 (10.74) | 51.15 (.96) |
| (4th) 1975-1979 | 573.75 (7.98) | (4.76) | 536.36 (7.46) | 1,037.50 (14.43) | 72.62 (1.01) |

SOURCE: The Bank of Korea, Economic Statistics Yearbook (Seoul, 1977) and The Bank of Korea, Monthly Economic Statistics (Seoul, January 1965-January 1980).

NOTE: Column (6) (technological effect) can be calculated as the residual of Equation 2 ($G_L + G_w/E_{LL} = G_k + (B_L + T)/E_{LL}$).

per annum (Table 7, column 3). This decreasing wage rate affected the positive labor absorption of 74.58 thousands of employment. Thus, the labor employment grew rapidly at 8.95% per annum in comparison with a capital stock growth rate of 5.44% in this period.

During the second period (1965-1970), the change in 243.40 thousands of annual average employment can be attributed to 578.87 thousands of the capital effect, 50.18 thousands of the technological effect, and a negative wage effect of 385.65 thousands of employment. From the beginning of this period, the real wage started to rise for the first time (see Figure 2), showing signs that Korea's unlimited supply of labor was approaching an end around 1966 (turning point). Therefore, the major capital effect of 578.87 thousands of employment and the minor effect of the technological progress (50.18 thousands of employment) can be offset by the amount of 385.65 thousands of employment caused by the effect of a drastic increase in real wage (8.12% per annum). Consequently, the increase in real wage was a causal determinant of the substitution of capital for labor after the turning point because Korea's entrepreneurs were induced to substitute capital for labor as labor became short and more expensive.

As a result, capital stock grew highly at a rate of 14.65% per annum during this period (1965-1970) in comparison with a rate of 5.44% during the prior period (1961-1965). At the same time, the rate of annual growth in employment ($G_L$) substantially decreased from 8.95% during the years 1961-1965 to 6.16% during the period (1965-1970). The combined technological progress, however, improved from .90% during the first period (1961-1965) to 1.27% during the second

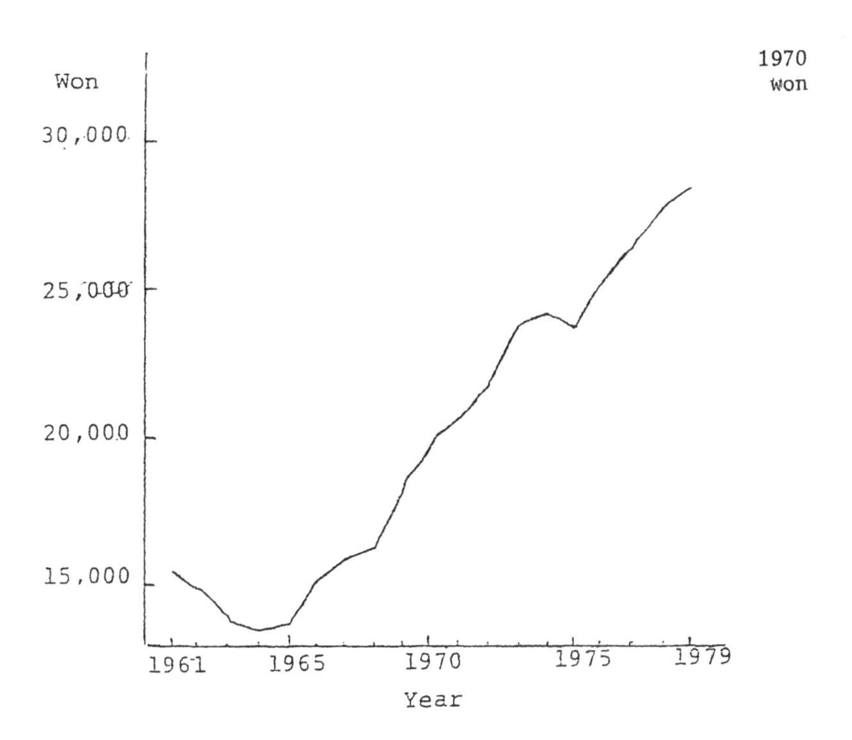


Fig. 2. Monthly real wage of nonagricultural sector (1961-1979).

period (1965-1970).

During the third and fourth periods (1970-1975 and 1975-1979), the annual rate of wage growth significantly dropped from 8.12% in the second period to 3.38% in the third period and to 4.76% in the fourth period. However, the real wage still increased so that the magnitudes of the capital effects (572.23 thousnads of employment in the third period and 1,037.50 thousands in the fourth period) and the technological effects (51.15 thousands of employment in the third period and 72.62 thousands in the fourth period) were absorbed by the wage effects (290.38 thousands of employment in the third period and 536.36 thousands in the fourth period). However, the changes in labor absorption (333.00 thousands of employment in the third period and 573.75 thousands in the fourth period) continually improved because capital stock continued to grow rapidly and, therefore, had a tremendous impact on the labor absorption, as compared with the combined technological effect during those periods.

Generally speaking, as presented in the figures of Table 7, the remarkable capital accumulation via domestic and foreign savings channels has played a major role in the labor absorption process, having great impact on the labor absorption in the Korean economy from 1961 to 1979. The combined technological progress (labor-biased technological progress), however, has played a relatively minor role in the labor absorption during the entire time period--wavering between .9% of the first period and a maximum (in the second period) of 1.27%.

Thus far, we have searched for the determinants of labor

absorption from the agricultural sector. The combined exogenous forces of capital accumulation and technological progress determined the rate of labor absorption in the nonagricultural sector. It is generally required for successful economic development that the nonagricultural sector absorb from the rural sector as much a redundant labor force as possible, and as soon as possible, under the combined pull of capital accumulation and technological progress.

However, there is another important factor in relation to this for a successful development effort in a less-developed economy. A population explosion has an adverse effect on industrialization. The high rate of population growth is a crucial factor offsetting the nation's economic development effort. If the rate of population growth exceeds the rate of labor absorption in the nonagricultural sector, then the pool of rural surplus population will be expanded by demographic pressures over time. The population pool in the rural sector never will dry up unless the withdrawal of surplus labor from this sector dominates population growth. Consequently, a shift in the economy's center of gravity toward industrialization cannot be expected without population control. This is illustrated by the "critical minimum effort analysis" of Professors Fei and Ranis who contend that:

> If a particular labor surplus economy is to meet the criterion of success as characterized by the fact that the center of gravity is shifting toward the industrial sector, the rate of increase of the industrial labor force must exceed the rate of growth of population.[5]

The condition of critical minimum effort is, therefore, given as a

---

[5]Ibid., p. 121.

growth rate of the nonagricultural labor force being higher than that of the population in the economy as follows:

$$G_L > G_p \tag{4}$$

where $G_L$ is the rate of growth of the nonagricultural labor force as mainly the combined forces of capital accumulation and technological progress, and $G_p$ the rate of population growth.

According to Korea's experience, the rates of growth of population, the nonagricultural labor force and the agricultural labor force can be observed in Table 8 and Figure 3. In every time period under discussion, the nonagricultural employment's rate of growth far exceeded that of the population, so that the critical minimum effort criterion has been satisfied in the Korean experience. The rates of population growth, as shown in Table 8, column 2, dramatically declined from 2.8% per annum in the first period (1961-1965) to 1.6% in the last period (1975-1979), and from 2.3% in the 1960s to 1.9% in the 1970s.

These figures were due to the fact that the government sponsored planned parenthood programs that aimed at a reduction of population growth in Korea. The government launched a family planning program (FPP) in 1962, whereby the natural rate of population growth was curtailed to 2.1% by 1971. Under the planned parenthood program, the government distributed free birth control devices such as intrauterine, vasectomy, condoms, and oral pills.[6]

---

[6]Lee-Jay Cho, Projections of the Population of the Republic of Korea (Honolulu: East-West Population Institute, 1976) and The Hapdon News Agency, Korean Annual (Seoul, 1979), p. 193.

TABLE 8

CRITICAL MINIMUM EFFORT ANALYSIS, 1961-1979
(Percent)

| (1)<br>Period<br>Annual Average | (2)<br>Population Growth Rate<br>($G_p$) | (3)<br>Nonagricultural Labor Force Growth Rate<br>($G_{NL}$) | (4)<br>Agricultural Labor Force Growth Rate (Inactive and Active Labor Force)<br>($G_{AL}$) |
|---|---|---|---|
| 1st 1961-1965 | 2.8 | 8.9 | -.6 |
| 2nd 1965-1970 | 2.1 | 6.1 | 1.3 |
| 3rd 1970-1975 | 2.0 | 6.2 | 1.6 |
| 4th 1975-1979 | 1.6 | 8.0 | .1 |
| 1961-1970 | 2.3 | 7.1 | .9 |
| 1970-1979 | 1.9 | 7.0 | .9 |
| 1961-1979 | 2.1 | 7.1 | .7 |

SOURCE: The Bank of Korea, Monthly Economic Statistics (Seoul, January 1965-January 1980) and Hapdong News Agency, Korean Annual (Seoul, 1965-1979).

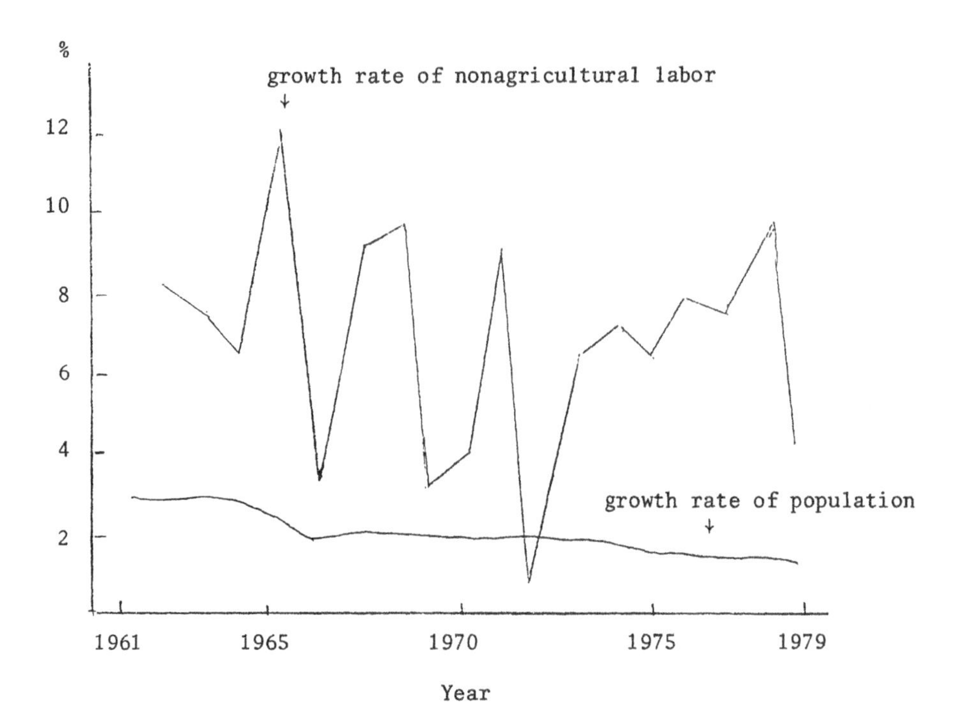


Fig. 3. The rates of growth of nonagricultural labor and population (1961-1979).

As a result, most housewives in the country were reported to favor this program and the traditional belief that many children are a blessing to parents has been gradually giving way to the need to control births to achieve a high standard of living. Thus, the program effectively achieved the birth control objective and brought down the annual rate of population growth from 2.9% in 1961 to 2.1% in 1971 and furtherdown to 1.6% in 1979.

The labor absorption in the nonagricultural sector, however, grew at a high annual rate of 8.9% in the first period (1961-1965). After the turning point (around 1966), the rate of growth of labor absorption suddenly dropped to 6.1% in the second period (1965-1970), slightly increased to 6.2% in the third period (1970-1975), and then to 8.0% in the fourth period (1975-1979).

These figures clearly indicate that Korea's development effort does indeed meet the criterion of critical minimum effort, namely that the rate of labor absorption in the nonagricultural sector consistently exceeded the rate of population growth during the years 1961-1979.

Now, let us illustrate the process of labor reallocation from the agricultural to the nonagricultural sector. The shift in center of economic gravity to the nonagricultural sector can be figured in terms of the rate of labor force growth in each sector and the percentage of total labor force active in the agricultural and nonagricultural sectors. That is, industrialization depends upon the fact that the percentage of total labor force allocated to nonagricultural activity increases through time.

Thus, we have evidence of the success of Korea's rapid industrial development caused by the process of labor reallocation during our study period. The nonagricultural labor force increased greatly at an annual average rate of 7.1% in the 1960s and at a rate of 7.0% in the 1970s. The agricultural labor force, however, has been negligibly increasing at less than 1% per annum in both 1960s and 1970s (Table 8, column 4).

The structure of total employment can be observed in Table 9. At the end of 1963, the percentage of total labor force allocated to the nonagricultural sector was 38.4%, while the percentage given to the agricultural sector was 61.6%. Between 1970 and 1971, the labor force became almost equally distributed to each sector. However, by 1979, the reverse of the 1963 situation had occurred to the point that 61.1% of the total labor force had been reallocated to the nonagricultural sector (Figure 4).

Thus, Korea's experience indicates that the rate of labor absorption by the nonagricultural sector has consistently dominated both the rate of population growth and the agricultural labor force's rate of growth during the entire period. Consequently, Korea's escape from the population explosion trap has been successfully achieved so that the reserved labor pool in the rural sector has quickly dried up to meet the criterion of Korea's development effort.

## Capital-Labor Ratio and Factor-Biased Technological Porgress

In short, we have examined Korea's capital growth and its labor absorption in the nonagricultural sector during our study period.

TABLE 9

STRUCTURE OF EMPLOYMENT, 1963-1979
(Percent)

| (1) Year | (2) Agricultural Sector | (3) Nonagricultural Sector | (4) Total Employment |
|---|---|---|---|
| 1963 | 61.6 | 38.4 | 100.0 |
| 1965 | 57.1 | 42.9 | 100.0 |
| 1970 | 51.4 | 48.6 | 100.0 |
| 1975 | 45.9 | 54.1 | 100.0 |
| 1979 | 38.8 | 61.1 | 100.0 |

SOURCE: The Bank of Korea, Economic Statistics Yearbook (Seoul, 1977) and The Bank of Korea, Monthly Economic Statistics (Seoul, January 1965-January 1980).

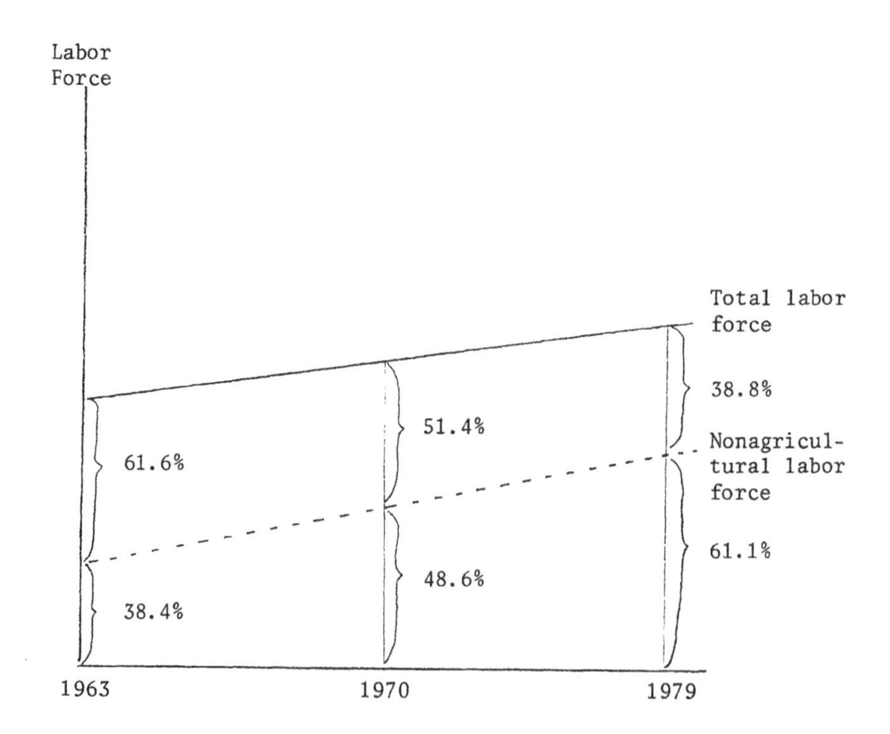


Fig. 4. Labor composition between agricultural and nonagricultual sector (1963-1979).

Table 10 helps summarize the rates of growth of capital and labor (columns 2 and 3) in relation to the growth of real wage (column 5).

One important characteristic of Korea's growth path in terms of capital-labor production technique is a tendency toward capital shallowing before the turning point (around 1966) which then yielded to capital deepening after that point, according to changes in real wage.

The growth path in Figure 5 illustrates a capital shallowing in the early 1960s (first period) and then a strong capital deepening tendency after 1965 through 1979.

The capital shallowing phenomenon (a reduction in capital-labor ratio, $G_{k/L}$: -3.51 in column 4) in the first period (1961-1965) indicates that Korea's economy more effectively used surplus labor under the condition of an unlimited supply of labor. The downward trend of real wage ($G_w$: -2.75% per annum) in this period should reflect an upward shift in demand for labor which represents a labor absorption increase of 8.95% per annum.

During the second period of 1965-1970, however, the real wage began to increase sharply at an annual rate of 8.12% which seems to signal the end of Korea's unlimited supply of labor. This means that the economic turning point was reached around 1966. At approximately the time of this turning point, the capital-labor ratio was sensitively increased from the first period rate of -3.51% to a second period rate of 8.49% per annum in the wake of increases in real wage. Once the real wage began to rise sharply, it was not surprising that capital immediately started to grow faster at an annual rate of 14.65%

TABLE 10

CAPITAL DEEPENING TENDENCY IN THE NONAGRICULTURAL SECTOR, 1961-1979
(Percent)

| (1) Period (Annual Average) | (2) Rate of Capital Growth ($G_k$) | (3) Rate of Labor Growth ($G_L$) | (4) Rate of Growth of K/L Ratio ($G_{k/L}$) | (5) Rate of Real Wage Growth ($G_w$) | (6) Labor-biased Technological Progress [$(B_L+T)/E_{LL}$] |
|---|---|---|---|---|---|
| (1st) 1961-1965 | 5.44 | 8.95 | -3.51 | -2.75 | .90 |
| (2nd) 1965-1970 | 14.65 | 6.16 | 8.49 | 8.12 | 1.27 |
| (3rd) 1970-1975 | 10.74 | 6.25 | 4.49 | 3.38 | .96 |
| (4th) 1975-1979 | 14.43 | 7.98 | 6.45 | 4.76 | 1.01 |

SOURCE: The Bank of Korea, Economic Statistics Yearbook (Seoul, 1977) and The Bank of Korea, Monthly Economic Statistics (Seoul, January 1965-January 1980).

NOTE: Column (6) is from Table 7, Column (6). Column (4) = Column (2) - Column (3) or $G_{k/L} = G_k - G_L$.

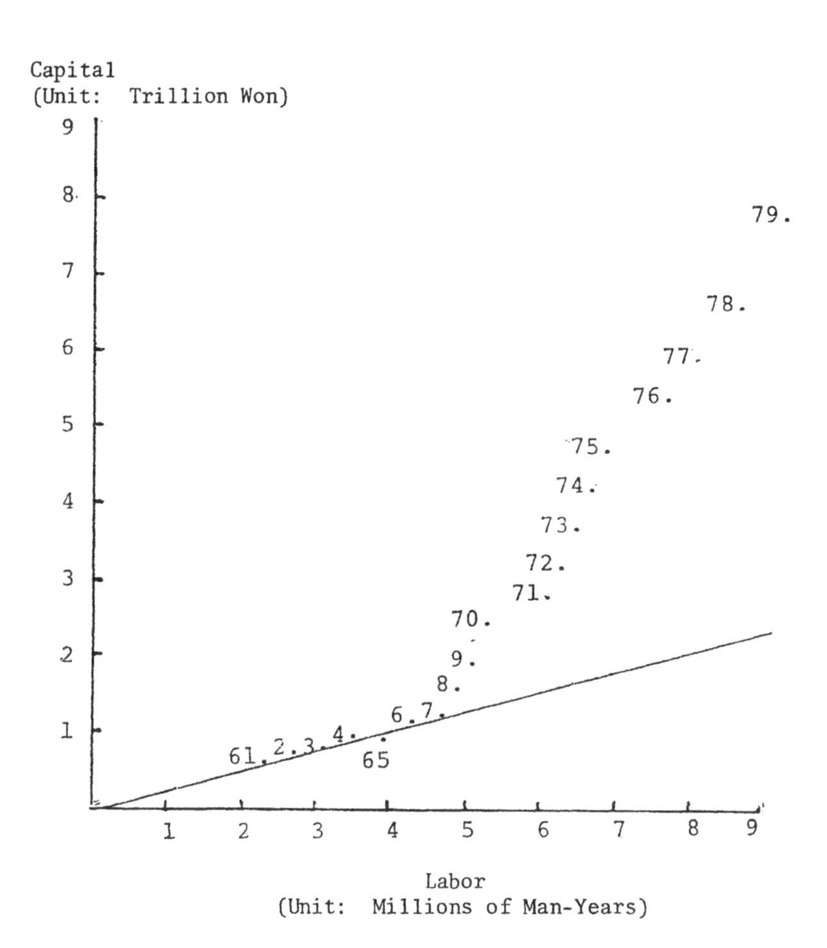


Fig. 5. Growth path (1961-1979).

relative to the labor growth rate of 6.16% during the second period. Thus, the capital-labor ratio dramatically increased at an annual rate of 8.49% during the second period (1965-1970). The reason is that profit-maximizing entrepreneurs were induced to substitute capital for labor as labor became relatively more expensive than capital after the turning point.

After the second period, the capital deepening tendency moderated to an annual growth rate of 4.49% in the third period and to 6.45% per annum in the fourth period as the real-wage growth rate declined in both periods.

Generally speaking, Korea's economy experienced a tendency toward capital shallowing in the early 1960s and then a reversal toward capital deepening from the turning point through 1979 in the course of increases in real wage. Thus, Korea's experience is consistent with the following theoretical framework:

$$G_{K/L} = \frac{G_w}{E_{LL}} - \frac{B_L + T}{E_{LL}} \qquad (5)^7$$

where the two terms on the right-hand side of the above equation can be regarded as the causal factors determining the rate of capital deepening. This equation states that, given technological progress, an increase in real wage immediately leads to an increase in capital-labor ratio.

In this equation, however, combined technological progress $[(B_L + T)/E_{LL}]$ depends upon changes in both real wage and capital-

---

[7] Equation 5 can be derived from Equation 2.

labor ratio grows faster than real wage in the above equation, the technological progress will inevitably result in a labor-saving direction in which the relative share of labor decreases.[8]

In other words, if an increase in real wage causes much faster growth in the capital-labor ratio, then the technological progress has a labor-saving direction in the developing economy.

Reaching the turning point, a developing economy is likely to substitute capital for labor as labor becomes scarce and more expensive. If a strong capital deepening takes place (resulting from immoderate capital growth in the wake of an increase in real wage), then technological progress will have an inevitable tendency to become increasingly labor-saving or very labor-saving. This is likely to take place in the course of improper capital-intensive industrialization in the developing economy.[9]

The empirical evidence on Korea's economy, presented in Table 10, indicates that the capital shallowing of the early 1960s yielded to a strong capital deepening tendency from the late 1960s through 1979. It is possible that this phenomenon led to labor-saving technological progress, especially during the third and fourth periods.

---

[8]John Richard Hicks, The Theory of Wages (London: McMillan and Co., 1935), pp. 121-127.

[9]A typical example is India's experience: During the period 1949-1960, India's wage inflation led to dramatic increase in the capital-labor ratio (a strong capital deepening) in her industrial sector. The effect of the high rate of growth on the capital-labor ratio through time resulted in a very labor-saving direction in the technological progress.

According to the figures in each period in Table 10, column 6, we cannot clearly distinguish the direction of technological progress until neutral technological progress T is estimated in the following chapters. However, we can roughly judge that the second period (1965-1970) was the best period for improving labor's position and that the labor share relative to capital was better in the 1960s than in the 1970s.

In summary, for the purpose of shifting Korea's economic center of gravity quickly from the agricultural to the nonagricultural sector, Korea has achieved successful capital accumulation in the nonagricultural sector by means of foreign capital inducement, domestic capital mobilization, and monetary expansion during the years 1961-1979.

Thus, the net fixed capital stock in the nonagricultural sector has dramatically grown at an annual average rate of 11.4% during the entire period under discussion. This remarkable capital growth has had a crucial impact on the successful transfer of surplus labor from the agricultural sector to the nonagricultural sector. Consequently, it has played a major role in the labor absorption in Korea's developing economy.

Therefore, the labor force in the nonagricultural sector grew substantially, at an annual rate of 7.2%, during the period 1961-1979. This meets the basic criterion of successful industrialization, namely that the rate of labor absorption consistently dominates both the rate of natural population growth (2.1% per annum) and the rate of growth of the agricultural labor force, which was less than

1% per annum (.7%).

As Korea's economic center of gravity has shifted toward nonagricultural activity, the rural reserved labor force has been gradually exhausted and the unlimited supply of labor finally came to an end in the mid-1960s. As a result of the early advent of the turning point around 1966, drastic increases in real wage naturally brought about the substitution of capital for labor in the production techniques, which in turn led to much faster increases in capital relative to labor.

Thus, capital shallowing before the turning point yielded to strong capital deepening after that point. This immoderate capital-intensive industrialization technique has inevitably brought about a labor-saving direction in the technological progress. Such a phenomenon has had a significant impact on the growth and distribution of income, a set of circumstances, which will be examined in detail in the following chapters.

# CHAPTER III

## THE EFFECT OF CHANGES IN FACTORS ON ECONOMIC GROWTH

Korea's economic growth over the last two decades (1961-1979) has been rapid. This growth has been accompanied by successful capital accumulation, significant labor transfer, and steadily improving technology. Thus, the overall national income has grown enormously at an annual average rate of 9.8% from 1961-1979. Such remarkable growth of national income has led to an improvement in the standard of living as a whole. However, it seems to have left a less equal distribution of income after 1970.

As the economic center of gravity shifted from the agricultural sector to the nonagricultural sector, the fixed capital stock in the nonagricultural sector drastically increased at an annual rate of 11.4% in comparison to an annual labor force growth rate of 7.1% during the years 1961-1979. Thus, the high growth rate of capital stock relative to labor obviously led to a capital-deepening industrialization in the nonagricultural production technique.

However, in the agricultural sector, which has a poor endowment of land, the total arable acreage began to fall in 1969 as more and more cultivated land was alienated to industrial and urban usage. Furthermore, the rural labor force became significantly transferred to nonagricultural activity so that the farm labor force (including nonactive labor force) grew at less than 1% per annum during the same period.

As a result, the real nonagricultural income grew seven fold from 1961 to 1979, while the agricultural income increased only two and one-half times during this same period. Thus, the economy (of capital-intensive industrialization, along with an inactive agricultural sector), underwent significant changes in its structure, both intersectorally and intrasectorally.

This chapter will investigate the growth of both sectors in relation to the growth of economic factors and their policy measures. It will also examine the change in the relative shares between the two sectors in the course of Korea's economic development.

## Korea's Agricultural Growth

In the literature of economic development theory, it is generally believed that a revolution in agricultural productivity must precede entry into industrial development. In the LDC's economy, a majority of the people live in the rural sector that performs the relatively large economic activity, as compared to the relatively small industrial sector. The role of the agricultural sector in this context is very important in fueling the expansion of the industrial sector by being the essential source of food, manpower, agricultural surplus capital (wage funds), and raw materials for the nonagricultural sector. It also serves as a major source of demand for industrial goods. Thus, economic development must begin with agricultural development which will gradually eliminate rural poverty through increases in agricultural productivity before a vigorous hope for progress can exist elsewhere.

However, as the center of economic gravity shifts from the agricultural sector to the nonagricultural sector, the country which has a poor natural resources endowment will, sooner or later, reach the limitation of further improvement in agricultural productivity. In the long run, gains in agricultural productivity, even if sustained at a high level for some time, will ultimately tend to decline in the course of the development process. This is due to the fact that the economy has been faced with a limited natural resource endowment and a significant labor transfer into the nonagricultural sector. Thus, additional agricultural efforts will lead to severe losses of potential economic gains as a whole, resulting from diminishing returns.

At this point, the correct policy is clearly not to continue expending economic resources on the agricultural sector, but to develop the potentialities offered by foreign trade. This policy, then, involves a turn to the export substitution (exports of labor-intensive manufactured goods) and the importation of primary products (foods and raw materials). Once the economy is dynamically moving toward trade, the developing economy will substantially ease its path and accelerate its pace of industrialization, such as a faster rate of expansion of industrial employment and output growth.

Korea's development experience, however, provides little evidence for this conventional theory. On the contrary, Korea's economy illustrates a process of export-oriented industrial development in the context of an open economy, thus leaving its agriculture lagging far behind the average of other sectors from the outset and requiring the importation of food early in the growth path. However, in the 1970s, the government began to turn its attention to the agricultural sector. In the winter of 1971-1972, the government launched the New Community Movement (Saemaul Undong) in order to make a major rural effort (partially spurred by evidence of a decline in rural political support in the 1971 election).

At its core, this movement was a local "self-help" effort led by local officials of the Ministry of Home Affairs. The government supported the construction of new local roads, bridges, and housing facilities. There was also a gradual shift in emphasis from the improvement in the quality of rural life to renewed efforts for improving agricultural productivity.

Agriculture, therefore, did not, in any way, lead to Korea's economic development in the early developing period. On the contrary, it not only lagged behind the industrial sector, but also was actually pulled along by the nonagricultural sector. Thus, Korea's economic development is an illustration of how a nonagricultural revolution can precede and help to bring about agricultural development rather than the reverse.

In contrast, the economy of Taiwan has progressed along the base of the conventional development theory. Taiwan initially attempted to extract increases in available productivity from the agricultural sector and then proceeded gradually to develop the nonagricultural sector by means of the agricultural supports.

Simply speaking, Korea's economic development was much more

industrially export-oriented, while Taiwan experienced more of an agriculturally oriented development. These two different economic development phenomena, as a matter of course, have led to different results in the structure of the economy, especially in growth and distribution, both intersectorally and intrasectorally.

As indicated earlier, in the course of Korea's industrialization, a rapid structural transformation has been made in the agricultural sector since 1960. In this process, the agricultural sector has been faced with several critical problems such as a drastic decrease in the food self-sufficiency rate and a substantial increase in the income disparity between the agricultural and nonagricultural sectors. Agricultural output (value added) increased 4% per year from 1961 to 1979, which is far below the growth rate of 11.5% in the nonagricultural sector.

More functionally, the agricultural sector has had to face such vicious side effects as:

1. A rural active labor force shortage resulting from a massive labor transfer into the industrial activity.
2. A drastic substitution of farm machinery for labor input.
3. A decline in cultivated land caused by increasing industrial-urban usage.
4. A lagging agricultural productivity.

This situation can be roughly analyzed in terms of the aggregate production process which is the relationship between output (value added) and inputs, combined with total productivity and the agricultural development policies.

Thus, the growth of agricultural production depends on changes in the principal factors of production (labor, capital, and land) in relation to policy measures and on the rate of technological change over time.

First of all, let us investigate the farm labor force phenomenon in relation to industrialization. As mentioned earlier, rapid industrial-urbanization, relying on tremendous capital accumulation, contributed to a high rate of labor-absorption in the non-agricultural sector. The rising demand for labor in the nonagricultural sector caused a heavy migration from the rural sector. One study indicates that approximately 400,000 rural people moved to urban areas every year during the 1960s and the early 1970s.[10] Consequently, the agricultural population has drastically decreased in spite of Korea's overall relatively high natural birth rate of 2.1% per annum during the past two decades.

Furthermore, the quality of farm labor deteriorated because the nonagricultural sector absorbed the better educated and more productive young people, leaving a high proportion of the aged and women on the farms. The proportion of workers aged 14 to 24 years in the rural labor force decreased from 27% in 1963 to 21% in 1976. The proportion of workers aged 50 years or more rose from 19% to 27% during the same period.[11]

---

[10] P. Y. Moon, "Selected Issue in the Impact of Industrialization on Agriculture in Korea," Journal of Rural Development, Vol. 3 (1977), p. 160.

[11] Ibid., p. 161.

The quantity of labor force actually used in agricultural activity drastically decreased after the economic turning point (1966), as shown in Table 11, column 2. Consequently, the shortage of farm labor force has become a serious problem, particularly during the peak season. As a matter of course, an increase in the farm-wage rate resulting from the shortage of agricultural labor has induced a substitution of capital for labor in the agricultural production technique. Thus, capital inputs (fixed and working capital) significantly increased while labor input was decreasing in the farm production.

For example, as shown in Table 12, the labor time per hectare of arable land decreased from 2,870 hours in 1965 to 1,750 hours in 1979, while the average horse power (HP) of farm machinery increased from .17 HP/hectare in 1965 to 1.54 HP/hectare in 1979. This substitution of farm machinery for the labor force has been accelerated by the low price of farm machinery relative to that of labor input, particularly in the late 1970s.

Regarding the decline in cultivated land, Korea probably had the lowest amount of arable land per head of farm population of any nation in the world in the early 1960s. Thus, the government attempted to exploit upland pasture, forest areas, and tideland by making them suitable for crops. This conversion, however, has been rendered substantially expensive because of the low productivity of such land. Accordingly, this acreage could not be rented out because prospective tenants could not earn enough on this land to take care of their own needs and to pay a significantly high rent to the owner.

TABLE 11

GROWTH RATES OF INPUTS TO AGRICULTURE, 1954-1973
(Percent)

| (1) Period | (2) Labor Actually Used | (3) Fixed Capital | (4) Current Working Capital | (5) Cultivated Land | (6) Total Input |
|---|---|---|---|---|---|
| 1954-1960 | 5.23 | .73 | 6.89 | .53 | 2.98 |
| 1960-1965 | .74 | 1.16 | 5.07 | 2.04 | 1.95 |
| 1965-1970 | -2.57 | .99 | 14.46 | .47 | 1.10 |
| 1970-1973 | -4.33 | 1.40 | 11.25 | -.77 | -.10 |

SOURCE: Adapted from Sung Hwan Ban, Pal Young Moon and D. H. Perkins, _Rural Development_ (1965-1976) (Cambridge: Harvard University Press, 1980).

TABLE 12

UTILIZATION OF AGRICULTURAL FACTOR INPUTS PER HECTARE OF ARABLE LAND, 1965-1979

| (1)<br>Year | (2)<br>Farm Machinery<br>(H.P./ha) | (3)<br>Labor Input<br>(1000 hrs/ha) |
|---|---|---|
| 1965 | 0.17 | 2.87 |
| 1970 | 0.35 | 2.32 |
| 1971 | 0.41 | 2.41 |
| 1972 | 0.46 | 2.28 |
| 1973 | 0.52 | 2.24 |
| 1974 | 0.63 | 1.76 |
| 1975 | 0.71 | 1.82 |
| 1976 | 0.88 | 1.80 |
| 1977 | 1.07 | 1.75 |
| 1978 | 1.34 | 1.70 |
| 1979 | 1.54 | 1.75 |

SOURCE: National Agricultural Cooperative Federation, *Agricultural Cooperative Yearbook* (Seoul, 1970-1980).

Furthermore, the major underlying reason why government land development was slow is that there was not much land left to develop. Therefore, the government, having little incentive to develop additional land, inevitably neglected agricultural modernization in the early period of development by overemphasizing industrial export substitution, thus, deviating from an intersectoral balanced growth path.

To make matters worse, the cultivated land was significantly alienated to nonfarm usage every year in the course of rapid urban-industrialization. Approximately 31,000 hectares of farm land have been transformed to industry-urban usage every year since 1968. Consequently, cultivated land decreased from 2.31 million hectares in 1970 to 2.21 million hectares in 1979, as shown in Table 13. Thus, these land saving and labor saving technologies have actively been introduced into agricultural operations in the rural sector in Korea since the late 1960s.

In this situation, one of the most important economic factors in an increase of agricultural production is the improvement in agricultural productivity. Changes in productivity can increase the total output attainable from given inputs through time in the production process. Thus, the increase in output is due only to changes in the quality of inputs occurring through time and not to any changes in the quantity of physical inputs.

In this connection, given the lack of significant technological improvement in agricultural productivity, it followed that simultaneous lack of an increase in either rural labor or amount of arable land

TABLE 13

CULTIVATED LAND, 1960-1979
(Unit: 1,000 hectares)

| (1) Year | (2) Paddy | (3) Nonpaddy | (4) Total |
|---|---|---|---|
| 1960 | 1,206.3 | 818.6 | 2,024.8 |
| 1966 | 1,287.1 | 1,006.0 | 2,293.1 |
| 1970 | 1,283.6 | 1,033.1 | 2,316.7 |
| 1975 | 1,276.6 | 963.1 | 2,239.7 |
| 1976 | 1,290.0 | 948.2 | 2,238.2 |
| 1977 | 1,303.1 | 928.1 | 2,231.2 |
| 1978 | 1,312.0 | 909.9 | 2,221.9 |
| 1979 | 1,311.0 | 896.1 | 2,207.1 |

SOURCE: The Hapdong News Agency, _Korean Annual_ (Seoul, 1970-1979); The Bank of Korea, _Economic Statistics Yearbook_ (Seoul, 1977); adapted from Sung Hwan Ban, et al., _Rural Development_ (1945-1975) (Cambridge: Harvard University Press, 1980), p. 81; and Ministry of Agriculture and Forestry, _Yearbook of Agriculture and Forestry_ (Seoul, 1980).

available resulted in the lack of a rise in farm output.

Therefore, it was desired that Korea's agricultural productivity would improve so that the agricultural sector could produce enough farm output for a large increase in the industrial demand for agricultural products (food). As the economic center of gravity shifted toward nonagricultural sector, agricultural productivity should have significantly risen so a relatively smaller fraction of the total labor force could support the entire economy.

Furthermore, an increase in farm output resulting from total productivity improvement would bring about a decrease in the price of food products. In this case, consumers would benefit from the low food prices. On the other hand, if the rate of decrease in price became lower than the rate of increase in farm production, farmers would also benefit from the increase in the productivity.

The increase in agricultural productivity can be accomplished through technological changes in the form of improved techniques and cultivation practices. Thus, crop rotation, pest control, seed breeding, fertilizer use, a better irrigation system, and high-yielding cash crops may represent the major potential sources of agricultural productivity increase in an economy of limited natural resources such as in Korea and Taiwan.

Korea's agricultural sector experienced a slow increase in productivity at an annual rate of 1.3% over its 1946 level during the period 1950-1974 (see Tables 14 and 15). Taiwan, however, experienced a substantial increase in productivity at an annual rate of 3.2% during the same period, which was about two and one-half times as large as

TABLE 14

INDEX OF AGRICULTURAL PRODUCTIVITY
(1946 = 100, 3-year Moving Average)

| (1) Year | (2) Taiwan | (3) Korea |
|---|---|---|
| 1946 | 100.0 | 100.0 |
| 1950 | 124.6 | 105.6 |
| 1951 | 122.4 | 94.5 |
| 1952 | 126.3 | 92.8 |
| 1953 | 139.4 | 97.3 |
| 1954 | 134.6 | 106.0 |
| 1955 | 136.0 | 103.1 |
| 1956 | 145.1 | 101.5 |
| 1957 | 156.6 | 101.0 |
| 1958 | 164.3 | 104.0 |
| 1959 | 162.8 | 102.6 |
| 1960 | 159.8 | 103.2 |
| 1961 | 170.0 | 103.5 |
| 1962 | 170.2 | 107.1 |
| 1963 | 181.3 | 111.8 |
| 1964 | 195.7 | 116.1 |
| 1965 | 210.9 | 122.8 |
| 1966 | 212.2 | 122.3 |
| 1967 | 209.7 | 124.0 |
| 1968 | 209.0 | 126.8 |
| 1969 | 209.6 | 130.7 |
| 1970 | 208.4 | 133.7 |
| 1971 | 222.3 | 133.0 |
| 1972 | 234.9 | 133.9 |
| 1973 | 248.9 | 139.1 |
| 1974 | 264.0 | 142.7 |
| 1975 | 277.9 | --- |

SOURCE: Column (2) adapted from: Yhi-Min Ho, Agricultural Development of Taiwan (1903-1960) (Nashville, Tenn: Vanderbilt University Press, 1966) and Shirley W. Y. Kuo, The Taiwan Success Story (1952-1979) (Boulder: Westview Press, 1981). Column (3) adapted from: Sung Hwan Ban, et al., Rural Development (1945-1975) (Cambridge: Harvard University Press, 1980).

TABLE 15

GROWTH RATES OF AGRICULTURAL TOTAL PRODUCTIVITY, 1950-1974
(Average annual rate, percent)

| (1) Period | (2) Taiwan | (3) Korea |
|---|---|---|
| 1950-1966 | 3.5 | 1.1 |
| 1966-1974 | 3.0 | 1.9 |
| 1950-1974 | 3.2 | 1.3 |

SOURCE: Data are from Table 14.

that of Korea.

Before the turning point (1966), Korea's agricultural sector had a slight increase in productivity at an annual rate of 1.1%, as compared to 3.5% in Taiwan from 1950 to 1966. Here, Taiwan's economy had already experienced the higher rate of expansion in agricultural productivity in the early period of development. However, Korea's economy had a relatively slow rate of expansion in agricultural productivity during the same period.

After the turning point, Korea's rate of productivity growth improved by 1.9%, which was still far behind Taiwan's 3.0%. Generally, Korea's economy experienced a low rate of expansion of agricultural productivity both before and after the turning point, as compared to the relatively higher rate of Taiwan's agricultural productivity, as depicted in Figure 6. It is certain, then, that Korea's slow growth in productivity would have substantially contributed to a slow growth in agricultural production, agricultural income, and in turn, to the shortage of food in the economy.

## Agricultural Trade

The low growth in agricultural products (resulting from the lagging growth in productivity) and the increasing industrial demand for agricultural products, naturally brought about a shortage of food, especially major grains (rice and barley). Therefore, there have been substantial increases in the importation of agricultural products in order to deal with the shortage of food. In addition, quite a large volume of grains has been shipped into Korea under the U.S. PL 480

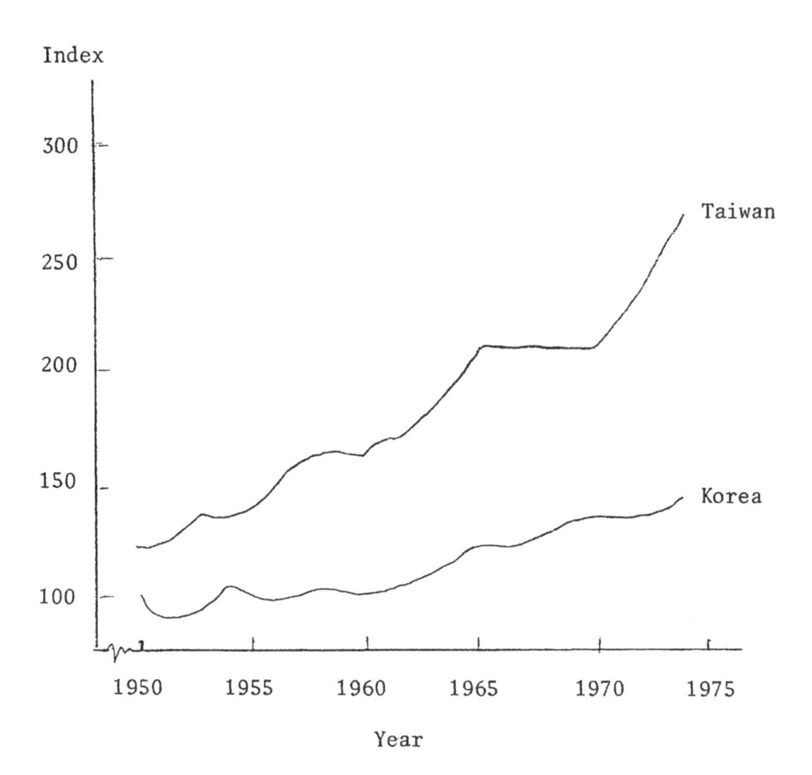


Fig. 6. Index of agricultural productivity (1964 = 100, 3-year moving average), 1950-1975.

grants-in-aid, in order to fill the food gap (Table 16).

It was worth noting that agricultural imports consistently exceeded agricultural exports, thus resulting in a considerable deficit in the agricultural trade account. The value of agricultural exports (in nominal terms) increased from 16 million dollars in 1960 to 1,356 million dollars in 1979, while the value of imported agricultural products increased from 91 million dollars in 1960 to 2,956 million dollars in 1979. Thus, agricultural imports consistently exceeded agricultural exports, so that the net imports increased significantly at an annual rate of 17.5% during the period 1960-1979 (Table 17).

As a consequence, the importation of agricultural products, including the PL 480 grains, contributed significantly to economic stability by maintaining grain prices at low levels. However, the availability of imported agricultural products undoubtedly reduced incentive to increase domestic agricultural production which, in turn, decreased farm output production and, thereby, reduced the self-sufficiency ratio of grains through time, as shown in Table 18.

## Grain Price Policy

As a result of the shortages of agricultural products, the government's grain policy was directed toward preventing large seasonal price fluctuations for major grains (rice and barley) through government purchases (domestic and foreign) and releases. Therefore, the Korean government, under the policy, had procured a considerable volume of rice and barley from domestic farmers, as well

TABLE 16

AGRICULTURAL IMPORTS UNDER U.S. PL 480, 1956-1980

| (1) Period | (2) Total PL 480 (million U.S. $) | (3) Grain Imports Under PL 480 (1,000 M/T) |
|---|---|---|
| 1956-1960 | 157.7 | 1,663 |
| 1961-1965 | 329.6 | 3,442 |
| 1966-1970 | 274.6 | 4,426 |
| 1971-1975 | 362.7 | 4,014 |
| 1976-1980 | 327.3 | 2,117 |

SOURCE: Ministry of Agriculture and Forestry, Yearbook of Agriculture and Forestry Statistics (Seoul, various years) and The Bank of Korea, Monthly Economic Statistics (Seoul, various years).

NOTE: Column (2) shows the amount of contracts made during each period and includes cereals, raw cotton and other nonfood farm products.

Column (3) shows the quantity of grains (including soybeans) actually delivered during each period.

TABLE 17

AGRICULTURAL EXPORT AND IMPORT, 1960-1979
(Unit: In million dollars)

| (1) Year | (2) Export (X) | (3) Import (M) | (4) Net Import (M-X) |
|---|---|---|---|
| 1960 | 15.6 | 90.6 | 75.0 |
| 1965 | 44.0 | 137.4 | 93.4 |
| 1970 | 138.1 | 488.3 | 350.2 |
| 1975 | 746.9 | 1,493.7 | 746.8 |
| 1978 | 1,224.6 | 2,146.6 | 922.0 |
| 1979 | 1,355.6 | 2,956.1 | 1,600.5 |

SOURCE: Economic Planning Board, *Economic Statistical Yearbook* (Seoul, 1963-1979).

TABLE 18

SELF-SUFFICIENCY RATIOS OF GRAINS, 1960-1979
(Percent)

| (1) Year | (2) Rice | (3) Barley | (4) Wheat | (5) Maize | (6) Soybean | (7) Others | (8) Total |
|---|---|---|---|---|---|---|---|
| 1960 | 100.8 | 110.4 | 33.9 | 18.9 | 79.3 | 100.0 | 94.5 |
| 1965 | 100.7 | 106.0 | 27.0 | 366.1 | 100.0 | 100.0 | 93.9 |
| 1970 | 93.1 | 106.3 | 15.4 | 18.9 | 86.1 | 100.0 | 80.5 |
| 1975 | 94.6 | 92.0 | 5.7 | 8.3 | 85.8 | 100.0 | 73.0 |
| 1976 | 100.5 | 97.9 | 4.5 | 6.7 | 74.4 | 100.0 | 74.1 |
| 1977 | 103.4 | 53.4 | 2.3 | 6.2 | 67.5 | 100.0 | 65.1 |
| 1978 | 103.8 | 119.9 | 2.1 | 6.0 | 59.3 | 100.0 | 72.6 |
| 1979 | 86.0 | 117.0 | 2.4 | 3.4 | 43.4 | 97.9 | 59.9 |

SOURCE: Ministry of Agriculture and Forestry, Yearbook of Agriculture and Forestry Statistics (Seoul, various years).

NOTE: Self-sufficency Ratio = domestic production/domestic consumption.

as foreign countries, in order to stabilize grain prices throughout the year.

The government acquired grain from farmers through various programs at government-prescribed prices during or after crop-harvest season. The major purchase programs included:

1. Direct purchases.
2. Barter of fertilizer for rice.
3. Rice-lien (nonrecourse loans).
4. Collection of farmland income taxes in kind.

However, the determination of government purchase prices and selling prices for rice and barley was closely related to such important aspects of the developing economy as rural income, urban consumer's welfare, the general price level, and a rural incentive for increased agricultural production.

A reduction in the grain prices for the urban consumers would result in a considerable decrease in rural household income, since rice and barley are a main source of farm income. This income loss might, in turn, cause farmers to reduce their use of inputs and, thus, adversely affect grain production, leading to a further reduction of farm income. The reduction of the grain purchasing price is not available, given the fact that grain production is less than domestic demand, which immediately brings about grain importation from foreign countries.

Conversely, a substantial rise in the grain prices for the rural farmers would cause unfavorable terms of trade in industrial goods and, in turn, lead to an increase in industrial wages via the consumer preference market mechanism.[12] This increase in industrial wages would not only place inflationary pressure (cost-push inflation) on the developing economy, but also reduce a stimulation of industrial labor absorption from the rural sector. This situation undoubtedly works against an industrial development policy in the developing economy.

Farmers tend to market most of their rice shortly after the rice harvests (November to January) when the rice price is usually low, as compared to that of off-seasons. This is because the demand for cash to pay debts or management expenses is generally concentrated in this period. Therefore, an adequate volume of government purchase is essential in order to maintain seasonal price stabilization by eliminating the excessive market supply during the harvest season.

In the early developing period (the 1950s), the government's primary efforts were placed on the rehabilitation of the war-torn economy and the alleviation of the inflationary spiral. Policy makers were particularly sensitive to the effects of grain prices on industrial development and the general price level. In this case, the government's

---

[12]Consumer Preference Market Mechanism. Assuming that the production functions of both agriculture and nonagriculture are subject to: 1) competitive market conditions, 2) homogeneity, and 3) hypothesis of Euler theorum. Here, factors are approximately paid each marginal product so that the total output is exhaustively distributed to the two classes of income recipients. Then: $W_A = MPP_{LA} \times P_A$, $W_N = MPP_{LN} \times P_N$, where W, MPP, and P are wage (nominal), marginal product of factor (real wage) and price, respectively. Under the competitive assumption, labor may be freely moveable between the two sectors, then: $W_A = W_N$, $MPP_{LA}/MPP_{LN} = P_N/P_A$, $w_A/w_N = P_N/P_A$ (terms of trade) where $w_A$ and $w_N$ are real wages in terms of their own goods, respectively. According to the terms of trade, a worsening of nonagricultural terms of trade caused by increases in agricultural price (shortage of grain) brings about an increase in nonagricultural real wage.

major emphasis was on maintaining low prices for urban consumers, rather than on farm income support. Therefore, the government purchase price of rice and barley remained lower than even the estimated costs of production almost every year until 1960 (Table 19). Here, the PL 480 shipments of grains played a significant role in maintaining grain prices at low levels. However, this low grain price policy caused serious income disparity between the farm and urban sectors, as well as discouraging grain production.

The Farm Products Price Maintenance Law was promulgated under the new military government in 1961. The objective of the law was to maintain proper prices of agricultural products in order to secure the stability of agricultural production and the rural economy. The government purchase prices for rice have exceeded the cost of production since 1961. However, these same prices were far lower than the market prices. This is because the new government's development strategy was still centered on rapid industrialization in the First Five-Year Economic Plan (1962-1966). The industrial sector received higher priority in sharing investment resources than the agricultural sector so that the industrial development strategy became particularly concerned about spiral inflation. Therefore, the farm price support continued to receive less attention as higher prices for grains were believed to cause not only a rise in cost-push inflationary pressure on the economy, but also a reduction in labor absorption from the agricultural sector.

As a result of drastic industrial expasion, agricultural production lagged far behind industrial production during the 1960s.

TABLE 19

GOVERNMENT PURCHASE PRICES, COST OF PRODUCTION, AND MARKET PRICES FOR RICE, 1950-1975
(Unit: In won per 80 kg.)

| (1) Year | (2) Purchase Prices | (3) Cost of Production | (4) Market Prices |
|---|---|---|---|
| 1950 | 16.40 | 15.88 | 52.30 |
| 1951 | 65.37 | n.a. | 157.50 |
| 1952 | 200.62 | 329.09 | 447.50 |
| 1953 | 200.62 | 330.94 | 350.00 |
| 1954 | 308.33 | 330.94 | 581.00 |
| 1955 | 390.56 | 838.44 | 962.00 |
| 1956 | 1,059.00 | 1,134.00 | 1,591.00 |
| 1957 | 1,059.00 | 1,384.00 | 1,311.00 |
| 1958 | 1,059.00 | 1,297.00 | 1,157.00 |
| 1959 | 1,059.00 | 1,300.00 | 1,368.00 |
| 1960 | 1,059.00 | 1,313.00 | 1,687.00 |
| 1961 | 1,550.00 | 1,377.00 | 1,768.00 |
| 1962 | 1,650.00 | 1,422.00 | 2,801.00 |
| 1963 | 2,060.00 | 1,373.00 | 3,470.00 |
| 1964 | 2.967.00 | 1,936.00 | 3,324.00 |
| 1965 | 3.150.00 | 2,672.00 | 3,419.00 |
| 1966 | 3,306.00 | 2,495.00 | 3,750.00 |
| 1967 | 3,590.00 | 2,735.00 | 4,289.00 |
| 1968 | 4,200.00 | 3,403.00 | 5,140.00 |
| 1969 | 5,150.00 | 3,565.00 | 5,784.00 |
| 1970 | 7,000.00 | 4,642.00 | 7,153.00 |
| 1971 | 8,750.00 | 4,682.00 | 9,844.00 |
| 1972 | 9,888.00 | 6,115.00 | 9,728.00 |
| 1973 | 11,377.00 | 6,578.00 | 12,175.00 |
| 1974 | 15,760.00 | 7,959.00 | 17,821.00 |
| 1975 | 19,500.00 | ---- | ---- |

SOURCE: Ministry of Agriculture and Forestry, _Grain Statistics Yearbook_ (Seoul, 1967-1975).

This led to an increase in food shortages, thus, triggering increased importation of grains and, at the same time, a growing income gap between urban and rural housholds.

In this situation, policy makers were obliged to give serious consideration to expanding food-grain production and to a more equitable income distribution between the two sectors.

The Two-Price System

In the 1970s, the government policy attempted to maintain a relatively high price level of grains so that the resulting high price of grain certainly would contribute to an increasing farm revenue, as well as to a saving in the foreign exchanges through both an increase in agricultural production and a reduction in agricultural importation.

However, high grain prices would cause an upward inflationary pressure and an adverse effect on both industrial labor absorption and urban consumer welfare. Here, a two-price grain system (a high price for farmers and a low price for urban consumers) was introduced as one means of resolving this economic intersectoral conflict.

The government attempted to maintain the consumer price at a level lower than producer support prices. As shown in Table 20, the selling prices have been, with the exception of 1971, considerably below the purchasing prices since 1970 (1969 for barley). For example, the government purchase price for rice in 1970 was 7,000 won per 80-kg bag, but the selling price was 6,500 won, which was lower than the purchase price by 500 won. (If the costs of handling rice were included, the deficit in government grain operations would be more

TABLE 20

THE TWO-PRICE SYSTEM FOR RICE AND BARLEY, 1961-1979
(Unit: In won per 80 kg.)

| (1) | (2) | (3) | (4) | (5) | (6) | (7) |
|---|---|---|---|---|---|---|
| | Rice | | | Barley | | |
| Year | Purchase Price | Selling Price | Difference (3-2) | Purchase Price | Selling Price | Difference (6-5) |
| 1961 | 1,550 | 1,792 | 242 | --- | --- | --- |
| 1962 | 1,650 | 1,888 | 238 | --- | --- | --- |
| 1963 | 2,060 | 2,312 | 252 | --- | --- | --- |
| 1964 | 2,967 | 3,450 | 483 | 1,147 | 1,377 | 230 |
| 1965 | 3,150 | 3,350 | 200 | 2,295 | 2,463 | 168 |
| 1966 | 3,306 | 3,900 | 594 | 2,295 | 2,463 | 168 |
| 1967 | 3,590 | 4,100 | 510 | 2,490 | 2,632 | 142 |
| 1968 | 4,200 | 5,200 | 1,000 | 2,640 | 2,750 | 110 |
| 1969 | 5,150 | 5,470 | 320 | 3,348 | 2,750 | -598 |
| 1970 | 7,000 | 6,500 | -500 | 3,850 | 3,100 | -750 |
| 1971 | 8,750 | 9,500 | 750 | 4,890 | 4,300 | -590 |
| 1972 | 9,888 | 9,500 | -388 | 6,357 | 4,800 | -1,557 |
| 1973 | 11,377 | 11,264 | -113 | 6,993 | 6,000 | -993 |
| 1974 | 15,760 | 13,000 | -2,760 | 9,091 | 6,900 | -2,191 |
| 1975 | 19,500 | 16,730 | -2,770 | 11,100 | 8,320 | -2,780 |
| 1976 | 23,200 | 19,500 | -3,700 | 13,000 | 9,200 | -3,800 |
| 1977 | 22,260 | 22,420 | -3,840 | 15,500 | 9,200 | -6,300 |
| 1978 | 30,000 | 26,500 | -3,500 | 18,500 | 10,120 | -8,380 |
| 1979 | 36,600 | 32,000 | -4,600 | 22,000 | 10,120 | -11,880 |

SOURCE: Ministry of Agriculture and Forestry, Yearbook of Agriculture and Forestry Statistics (Seoul, various years).

than that.)

Thus, the two-price grain policy through the government price subsidy might have contributed to increasing consumers' and producers' welfare, to increasing industrial labor absorption, and to alleviating cost-push inflationary pressure on the economy. However, the deficit in government grain management has been significantly accumulated since 1970. The implementation of the two-price grain policy caused the actual financial losses the government incurred, due to the grain price subsidies. In this case, the impact of the government financial losses on the overall economy depended upon how the deficit was financed, such as the source of financing. This grain deficit could be financed from the general budget account in every fiscal year, thus preventing inflationary effect. However, the grain deficit account was actually financed by overdrafts from the central bank which was a means of money supply (revenue from an inflation tax).

According to Table 21, the change in the money supply, due to the grain deficit, resulted in significant monetary expansion during the period 1970-1975. It accounted for 22.3% of the total increase in money supply in 1972, 23.7% in 1973, 74.3% in 1974, and 98.2% in 1975. This implied that nearly all the increase in money supply resulted from new money creation due to the grain deficit account, especially in 1974 and 1975.

The grain management deficit obviously had a negative effect on the stability of price level, so far as it was deficit-financed by monetary expansion. However, it should be noted that the grain manage-

TABLE 21

THE EFFECT OF GRAIN DEFICIT ON MONEY SUPPLY, 1970-1975
(Unit: In billion won)

| (1) Year | (2) Overdraft | (3) Repayment | (4) Balance | (5) Outstanding Balance | (6) Total Money Supply | (7) Change In Money Supply | (8) (4)/(7) (%) |
|---|---|---|---|---|---|---|---|
| 1970 | 2.0 | 2.0 | 0 | 0 | 307.6 | 55.6 | --- |
| 1971 | 0 | 0 | 0 | 0 | 358.0 | 50.4 | --- |
| 1972 | 50.0 | 14.0 | 36.0 | 36.0 | 519.4 | 161.4 | 22.3 |
| 1973 | 50.0 | 0 | 50.0 | 86.0 | 730.3 | 210.9 | 22.3 |
| 1974 | 160.0 | 0 | 160.0 | 246.0 | 945.7 | 215.4 | 74.3 |
| 1975 | 231.7 | 0 | 231.7 | 477.7 | 1,181.7 | 236.0 | 98.2 |

SOURCE: Ministry of Agriculture and Forestry, *Yearbook of Agriculture and Forestry Statistics* (Seoul, various years) and The Bank of Korea, *Economic Statistics Yearbook* (Seoul, 1970-1976).

ment deficit also had some favorable effects on the economy. The maintenance of government selling prices of grain at a lower than equilibrium level certainly contributed to the stabilization of consumer's grain prices. At the same time, producers' price support, through the deficit account, stimulated a domestic production of grains, and this increased production further contributed to the stabilization of grain prices and also to the savings of a considerable amount of foreign exchange.

Furthermore, it is worth noting that the deficit in government grain operations had a significant effect on the distribution of income between rural and urban households. As illustrated by the data on the terms of trade in Table 22, the average prices paid to farmers were generally below the average prices paid by famers during the 1960s. Therefore, the terms of trade had been roughly unfavorable for the rural sector until 1970 when the government's grain policy underwent a marked change by adopting a high price policy for grains through the two-price system. Consequently, the terms of trade moved in favor of the agricultural sector until 1975, mainly due to the high grain price policy operating since 1970.

According to the intersectoral comparison of household income as shown in Table 23, the income differential was of comparable significance to the farm households between the 1960s and the early 1970s. The differential moved substantially in favor of urban households from the early 1960s to the late 1960s. However, the situation gradually reversed in favor of rural households, during the early half of the 1970s, due to the two-price system.

TABLE 22

TERMS OF TRADE FOR AGRICULTURAL PRODUCTS, 1961-1975
(1970 = 100)

| (1)<br>Year | (2)<br>Index of Prices<br>Received by Farmers | (3)<br>Index of Prices<br>Paid by Farmers | (4)<br>(2)/(3) |
|---|---|---|---|
| 1961 | 24.6 | 28.7 | 85.7 |
| 1962 | 27.1 | 31.8 | 85.2 |
| 1963 | 40.1 | 35.3 | 113.6 |
| 1964 | 50.2 | 44.8 | 112.1 |
| 1965 | 52.2 | 51.8 | 100.8 |
| 1966 | 55.4 | 58.1 | 95.4 |
| 1967 | 63.5 | 65.8 | 96.5 |
| 1968 | 74.3 | 78.8 | 94.3 |
| 1969 | 84.8 | 86.8 | 97.7 |
| 1970 | 100.0 | 100.0 | 100.0 |
| 1971 | 121.4 | 114.4 | 106.1 |
| 1972 | 147.9 | 130.5 | 113.3 |
| 1973 | 164.2 | 143.1 | 114.7 |
| 1974 | 215.6 | 192.5 | 112.0 |
| 1975 | 267.6 | 237.9 | 112.5 |

SOURCE: Same as Table 21.

TABLE 23

COMPARISON OF HOUSEHOLD INCOMES BETWEEN RURAL AND URBAN, 1963-1975
(Unit: In current price won)

| (1) Year | (2) Rural Yearly Income per Household | (3) Urban Yearly Income per Household | (4) Ratio (2)/(3) |
|---|---|---|---|
| 1963 | 82,799 | 80,160 | 1.03 |
| 1967 | 138.718 | 248,640 | 0.56 |
| 1970 | 230,170 | 381,240 | 0.60 |
| 1974 | 465,794 | 644,520 | 0.72 |
| 1975 | 722,716 | 589,320 | 0.84 |

SOURCE: Ministry of Agriculture and Forestry, Report on the Results of Farm Household Economic Survey (Seoul, various issues) and Economic Planning Board, Annual Report on the Family Income and Expenditure Survey (Seoul, 1975).

Generally speaking, the grain price policy for industrialization was directed toward maintaining low prices for urban workers and preventing large seasonal price fluctuations. Thus, in order to alleviate wage inflation and to increase absorption of rural labor force, the government attempted to maintain low grain prices by the importation of foreign grains from the beginning of the development period. Therefore, the low grain price policy discouraged an increase in agricultural production and self-sufficiency, thereby causing considerable income inequality between the rural and urban sectors.

Land Reform

Korea has a long history of absentee landlords, where tenant farmers suffered from feudalistic landlords. The feudalistic tenure system was characterized by extremely unfavorable terms of tenure and the subordinate social status of tenants to landlords. This system intensified during the Japanese Colonial Period (1910-1945) and did not improve immediately after liberation.

In December 1945, approximately 60% of all cultivated land was under tenant farming and at least 50% of farm households were full-time tenants, while 4% of farm households owned 50% of all cultivated land.[13] Furthermore, it was common practice to charge approximately 50% to 70% of output as rent, despite the low productivity of land, as compared to today's productivity. Such high rates

---

[13]Eddy Lee, "Eglitarian Peasant Farming and Rural Development: The Case of South Korea," World Development, Vol. 7 (1979), p. 497.

of rent were possible because of the high man/land ratio in rural villages and the few opportunities for nonfarm employment in the country.

This adverse resource endowment, combined with a harsh tenancy system, unequal distribution of land, and a high rate of surplus extraction, resulted in conditions of widespread and extreme rural poverty and also threatened political stability. Therefore, the Korean government began to alleviate rural poverty through the consolidation of land. The land reform was introduced in 1948. However, due to controversies involved, the full scale implementation began only five years after liberation.

The objective of the reform was to improve farmer's standards of living and to ensure a balanced development of the national economy through increased agricultural productivity. However, the enactment of the land reform was promoted mainly by the political urgency to lay foundations for a free democracy. The main features of the land reform were:

1. Land to the tillers.
2. No tenant farming.
3. A three-hectare upper limit on the farmland ownership.

This land reform may be evaluated today as quite successful in an equity sense. There is no question that land reform caused a substantial shift in the direction of a greater owner-operator system from that of landless tenants, as shown in Table 24.

According to the distribution of farm households in farming size (Table 25), the proportion of farms with 1.0 hectare and below,

TABLE 24

COMPARISON OF FARM HOUSEHOLD BY CATEGORY OF TENURE, 1945-1977
(Percent)

<table>
<tr><th>(1)<br>Year</th><th>(2)<br>Landless<br>Tenant</th><th>(3)<br>Tenant<br>Owner</th><th>(4)<br>Owner<br>Tenant</th><th>(5)<br>Owner<br>Operator</th><th>(6)<br>Total</th></tr>
<tr><td>1945</td><td>51.6</td><td>18.2</td><td>16.4</td><td>13.8</td><td>100.0</td></tr>
<tr><td>1957</td><td>4.0</td><td colspan="2">8.0</td><td>88.0</td><td>100.0</td></tr>
<tr><td>1965</td><td>7.0</td><td>8.0</td><td>15.5</td><td>69.5</td><td>100.0</td></tr>
<tr><td>1970</td><td>9.7</td><td>7.8</td><td>16.0</td><td>66.5</td><td>100.0</td></tr>
<tr><td>1975</td><td>8.0</td><td>6.5</td><td>13.3</td><td>72.2</td><td>100.0</td></tr>
<tr><td>1977</td><td>6.6</td><td>9.4</td><td>20.1</td><td>63.9</td><td>100.0</td></tr>
</table>

SOURCE: Adapted from: Ho-Shung Oh, Economic Development and Land System (Korea) (Seoul, 1980).

NOTE: Tenant-owner denotes someone whose land under tenancy accounts for more than 50% of his total land holding, while owner-tenant means someone who had less than 50% of land under tenancy.

TABLE 25

DISTRIBUTION OF FARM HOUSEHOLDS BY SIZE OF FARM, 1947-1970
(Percent)

| (1)<br>Size of Farm | (2)<br>1947<br>(Before Land Reform) | (3)<br>1953<br>(After Land Reform) | (4)<br>1960 | (5)<br>1970 |
|---|---|---|---|---|
| Below 1 ha. | 74.5 | 79.1 | 73.0 | 67.7 |
| 1.0-2.0 ha. | 18.8 | 16.5 | 20.7 | 25.8 |
| Over 2.0 ha. | 6.7 | 4.4 | 6.3 | 6.5 |

SOURCE: Ministry of Agriculture and Forestry, Yearkbook of Agriculture and Forestry Statistics (Seoul, various years) and National Agricultural Cooperative Federation, Twenty-Year History of Korean Agriculture (Seoul, 1965), p. 99.

increased from 74.5% of the total in 1947 (before land reform) to 79.1% in 1953 (after land reform) and thereafter, dropped to 73.0% in 1960 and further to 67.7% in 1970.

On the contrary, the number of farms with one to two hectares dropped slightly from 18.8% in 1947 to 16.5% in 1953 and then increased to 20.7% in 1960 and to 25.8% in 1970. The proportion of farms above two hectares decreased right after the land reform and then returned to the same level as before the land reform.

Generally speaking, the proportions of farms of less than one hectare, between one and two hectares, and over two hectares, decreased, increased, and remained the same, respectively after the land reform. Thus, the small-sized farming groups decreased, the medium-sized farming households increased, and the large sized households stayed the same after 1953.

Here, the key issue was whether there were pronounced economies or diseconomies of scale in each farm size operation. The small-sized farm households with a large family membership could not earn enough on their small acreage to support their own family and pay annual compensation for land purchase to the landlords. Therefore, they left the farming villages for industrial urban sectors.

On the other hand, the large-sized farming groups could not cultivate even their own land with traditional cultivation techniques under conditions of "no tenant farming" and "a three hectare upper limit on farmland ownership."

However, the middle-sized farming households could have enough capacity to cultivate more land in their own family farming operation than they had. Therefore, these households increased by purchasing land from the small-sized farming groups after the land reform.

Now, two key issues were whether the land reform promoted or held back increases in agricultural productivity and whether the reform succeeded in redistributing rural income through equitable land ownership.

The land reform, however, did not bring about immediate increases in agricultural production, even though it created new incentives for farmers. For example, the production of rice averaged 1,820 kg per hectare during 1945-1949 and the five year average for 1950-1954 was 1,840 kg per hectare, showing an increase of only about 20 kg.[14]

This land reform did not seem to increase productivity as expected because rapid industrial growth, as mentioned earlier, transformed the agricultural structure drastically. As a result, this sector recently suffered from such problems as shortages of workers, technical substitution of farm-machine for labor-shortages, and inefficient farm-mechanization under the condition of "a three-hectare upper limit."

Under these circumstances, the current land tenure system appears to be increasingly inadequate in the sense that it imposes many legal restrictions on possible structural adjustments in the course of industrialization. This is because such salient features of land reform, as the three-hectare ceiling on land holding and the prohibition of tenant farming, are still in effect. Moreover,

---

[14]Korea Land Economic Research Center (KLERC), A Study of Land Tenure System in Korea (1966), p. 103.

cooperative farming also has no legal prospects of existence under the current system of land tenure. Consequently, Korea's agricultural sector experienced a slow growth in productivity at an annual rate of 1.3% over its 1946 level after the land reform as shown in Table 15.

In this relation, the inefficient farming management resulting from the lack of structural adjustments has continued to prevail in agricultural production. This caused a significant different in the rates of productivity growth between agricultural and nonagricultural sectors, which in turn, led to a growing income disparity between the two sectors due to the land tenure system.

It is, therefore, suggested that the current land system, which imposes a three hectare ceiling on farm size and prohibits tenancy, should be relaxed to allow easier structural adjustments to the changing economic development.

In sum, as a result of the vicious effects caused by the policy oriented rapid industrialization, Korea's agricultural sector became atrophied in agricultural modernization. Thus, the agricultural sector failed in its major role to become an essential source of food, raw materials, and agricultural surplus capital for the industrial sector. The agricultural sector did, however, achieve its role of providing manpower.

Rapid industrialization at the expense of agricultural modernization from the beginning of the development period is inconsistent with an intersectoral balanced growth path in developing countries. Professors Fei and Ranis illustrated this situation precisely when they commented in their work:

> An idealized intersectoral balanced growth path may then be characterized by a constancy in terms of trade. In this case, the expansion of the industrial capital stock on the one hand, and the expansion of agricultural productivity on the other, occurred in a balanced fashion so that the employment equilibrium points trace out a locus satisfying the condition of constant real wage. Along such a balanced growth path, the employment of labor gradually shifts from the agricultural to the industrial sector. This is "ideally" how the unemployment problem is solved in the dualistic economy.[15]

According to the above statement, the industrial capital growth must be harmonized with agricultural development in a fine-tuned fashion so that, first of all, the improved agricultural productivity leads to stabilized food prices and the subsequent stabilization of industrial terms of trade in the development process. Those stable terms of trade will continually curb wage-inflation in the nonagricultural sector via consumer's preference market forces between agricultural and nonagricultural goods, and will simultaneously stimulate labor absorption in the same sector (see previous chapter).

From the early period of development, however, Korea's economy experienced an intersectoral unbalanced growth path in the sense that the improper capital-intensive industrialization preceded Korea's potential agricultural modernization.[16] As a consequence of capital-biased

---

[15]John C. M. Fei and Gustav Ranis, "Development and Employment in the Open Dualistic Economy," American Economic Review (October 1971), p. 102.

[16]The Korean Government mobilized domestic savings, foreign borrowings, and even the revenue from an inflation tax by monetary expansion and then subsidized massive credits of those financial resources to preferred industries at low interest rates, as compared to the existing high rates of inflation. Consequently, this financial policy for industrialization resulted in a high increase in entre-

industrialization in the face of inadequate agricultural participation, the economy also experienced a relatively earlier economic turning point (around 1966) than usual, after which the wage inflation necessarily accelerated in the developing economy.

Thus, Korea's economy was forced to raise industrial wages relatively faster and earlier than usual. In this connection, the government continued to import a large volume of foreign grains and to directly control grain prices less than the cost of domestic production (before 1961) and domestic market prices (before 1970) in order to alleviate industrial wage inflation and to stimulate industrial labor absorption.

The vicious effects (agricultural labor shortages, technically inefficient substitution of farm machinery for labor, and decline in cultivated land by increasing urban industrial usages) caused by rapid industrialization and some unfavorable agricultural policies (continuous food importation, the low grain price policy, and the fixed land tenure system) definitely led to a lack of incentive for the agricultural sector, not only to increase agricultural production, but also to enhance agricultural modernization.

---

preneurs' profit between the low interest rate and the high rate of inflation. In this situation, profit maximizing entrepreneurs were further induced to substitute capital for labor after the economic turning point where the unlimited supply of labor became exhausted, so that it increased industrial wage levels. From the theoretical point of view at this point, capital and wage became so closely dependent on each other that every increase in capital directly fed a corresponding increase in wages. In turn, every increase in wage level immediately fueled an additional increase in capital. Such a spiral acceleration was generated, whereby Korea's industrial capital has been dramatically and improperly increased at an annual rate of 11.4% during the past two decades.

This situation also caused a relatively slow growth in agricultural productivity and, thus, a relatively greater decline in agriculture's share of national income from 38% in 1961 to 18% in 1979, as shown in Table 26. The reason for this drastic decline is that the nonagricultural sector had grown faster (at an annual rate of 11.5%) than the agricultural sector did (at an annual rate of 4.2%).

Thus, Korea's rapid economic growth (9.8% per annum), attributable to the remarkable expansion of the nonagricultural sector, has caused significant structural changes within and between the sectors. As a consequence of the high industrial growth, along with an inadequate agricultural participation, the economy had to face such serious problems as a decreasing food self-sufficiency and a widening income disparity between agricultural and nonagricultural sectors, as shown previously in Table 23.

The next section will investigate the growth of the nonagricultural sector in terms of the growth of economic factors. The functional distribution and shares of productivity gains between capital and labor also will be examined in relation to the growth of economic factors in the same sector.

## Sources of Nonagricultural Growth

Chapter II examined the growth of factor inputs and a direction of technological progress in the nonagricultural sector in relation to the agricultural sector. Agricultural development in terms of changes in input factors, productivity growth, and some policy measures have also been investigated in the early part of this chapter.

TABLE 26

DISTRIBUTION OF NATIONAL INCOME BETWEEN AGRICULTURAL AND NONAGRICULTURAL SECTOR, 1961-1979
(Unit: In billion 1970 won)

| (1) Year | (2) National Income (y) | (3) Agricultural Income (a) | (4) Nonagricultural Income (v) | (5) Agricultural Share ($S_a$) | (6) Nonagricultural Share ($S_v$) | (7) Relative Share ($S_a/S_v$) |
|---|---|---|---|---|---|---|
| 1961 | 1,055.42 | 400.52 | 654.90 | .379 | .621 | .610 |
| 1962 | 1,061.40 | 357.06 | 704.33 | .336 | .664 | .506 |
| 1963 | 1,174.29 | 468.32 | 705.98 | .339 | .661 | .513 |
| 1964 | 1,296.63 | 552.28 | 744.35 | .426 | .574 | .742 |
| 1965 | 1,354.28 | 471.58 | 882.70 | .348 | .652 | .534 |
| 1966 | 1,500.27 | 484.58 | 1,015.69 | .323 | .667 | .484 |
| 1967 | 1,599.27 | 441.40 | 1,157.87 | .276 | .724 | .381 |
| 1968 | 1,761.19 | 448.08 | 1,313.09 | .254 | .746 | .340 |
| 1969 | 2,025.73 | 527.13 | 1,498.60 | .260 | .740 | .351 |
| 1970 | 2,256.25 | 548.08 | 1,708.17 | .243 | .757 | .321 |
| 1971 | 2,496.62 | 615.31 | 1,881.31 | .246 | .754 | .326 |
| 1972 | 2,657.75 | 644.84 | 2,012.92 | .243 | .757 | .321 |
| 1973 | 3,127.51 | 699.51 | 2,427.99 | .224 | .776 | .289 |
| 1974 | 3,494.55 | 796.15 | 2,698.41 | .228 | .772 | .295 |
| 1975 | 3,663.39 | 862.41 | 2,800.98 | .235 | .765 | .307 |
| 1976 | 4,222.88 | 959.43 | 3,263.44 | .227 | .773 | .294 |
| 1977 | 4,564.44 | 961.30 | 3,603.13 | .211 | .789 | .276 |
| 1978 | 5,135.42 | 1,028.95 | 4,106.47 | .200 | .800 | .250 |
| 1979 | 5,688.63 | 1,033.74 | 4,654.89 | .182 | .818 | .222 |
| Growth Rate (%) | 9.8 | 4.2 | 11.5 | | | |

SOURCE: The Bank of Korea, Economic Statistics Yearbook (Seoul, 1977) and The Bank of Korea, Monthly Economic Statistics (Seoul, Jan. 1965-Jan. 1981).

NOTE: All incomes (factor costs) are deflated by GNP deflator based on 1970 won.

Nonagricultural income is functionally classified into wage and property income, but agricultural income is not.

This paper will now investigate functional input-output relations in the nonagricultural sector, meaning the effects of changes in capital, labor, and technology on the nonagricultural growth. This study will then relate the growth to the distribution of income in the production process.

As demonstrated in Table 26, Korea's nonagricultural sector achieved one of the highest growth rates (11.5% per annum) in the world during the 1961-1979 period. It is possible that one of the most interesting questions concerning the remarkable growth of the nonagricultural sector is the extent to which various economic factors contributed to the growth in output. This approach can be followed by examining changes in capital, labor, and technology or more precisely, the disparity between the increments in inputs (capital and labor) and output.

For this analysis, the aggregate production function can be illustrated by Professor Solow's equation as follows:[17]

$$V = f\ (K, L, t) \qquad (6)$$

where V, K, L, and t are output, capital, labor, and time, respectively.

In the special case where technological change is assumed to be neutral[18] (that is, the marginal rates of factor substiution are

---

[17]Robert M. Solow, "Technical Change and the Aggregate Production Function," Review of Economic Statistics, Vol. 39 (August 1957), pp. 312-320.

[18]Solow's neutral technological change refers to any kind of shifts in the production function. It combines all factors influencing

not affected by shifts in the production function), the above production function can be rewritten as:

$$V = T(t)\ f(K,L). \qquad (7)$$[19]

In an attempt to obtain a growth equation model from the production function, one may differentiate the production function totally with respect to time and divide by V. Then, one will readily have a differential equation in the following fashion:

$$\frac{\dot{V}}{V} = \frac{\dot{T}}{T} + b\frac{\dot{K}}{K} + a\frac{\dot{L}}{L} \qquad (8)$$

$$(G_V = G_T + b\ G_K + a\ G_L)$$

where $\dot{V}/V$ : $G_V$ (output growth rate),

$\dot{T}/T$ : $G_T$ (growth rate of technology),

$\dot{K}/K$ : $G_K$ (growth rate of capital),

$\dot{L}/L$ : $G_L$ (growth rate of labor),

b : capital share,

and a : labor share.

From Equation 8, it appears that sources of growth in nonagricultural output (value added) can be attributable to changes in

---

output other than changes in the quantity of capital and labor. Thus, Solow's technological progress is broadly defined.

[19]The following three assumptions are implicitly made in the production function: 1) The aggregate production function is linearly homogeneous of degree one by virtue of Euler's theorum. 2) Factors are approximately paid their marginal products (for instance, factor markets are competitive), and 3) neutral technological progress.

capital, labor, and technology through time. Here, technological change is not a tangible factor, but a time concept.[20] It combines all factors affecting output, other than changes in the quantity of capital and labor. Therefore, technological progress can be calculated as residual growth not explained by the growth of capital and labor inputs.

In this connection, the neutral technological change and the total factor productivity are identical in terms of an intangible factor through time in the production function. They both can be calculated in the same way as the ratio of real output (value added) produced to the aggregate input employed.[21] Thus, the total productivity is the divergence in the growth of output relative to the growth of the combined factor inputs, simply the ratio of output to the aggregate input.

For an attempt to calculate the total factor productivity (intangible factor), the question is how to measure the aggregate input from different physical units of inputs (capital and labor). For this calculation, the geometrical formula may be used for the aggregate input index as follows:

$$I_{kL} = I_k^b \, I_L^a \tag{9}$$

where $I_{kL}$ : aggregate input index of year t in relation to base year t = o,

---

[20]Time is regarded as a proxy variable for technological change.

[21]Under the assumption of the special case of neutral technological change in the production function, T(t) = V/f(K,L) = real output/aggregate input.

$I_k^b$ : capital input index weighted by capital share b from observed factor shares each year.

and $I_L^a$ : labor input index weighted by labor share a in the same way.

The aggregate input index, as compiled from the preceding formula is shown in Table 27. Indices of output (value added) and individual inputs are also shown in the same table. As mentioned earlier in this section, changes in output are brought about either by changes in inputs used or by total factor productivity change, or by both. The aggregate input index is simply the output index in the absence of the total factor productivity change broadly defined. The average rate of increase in the expected aggregate output (aggregate input index) comes to 8.6% per year during the 1961-1979 period, as shown in Table 27, column 5. Capital input (index) and labor input (index) increased at 11.4% and 7.2% per annum, respectively, during the same period, as shown in Table 27.

The rate of growth in the aggregate input (index) was attributable to increases in capital input and labor input through time. Thus, of the 8.6% annual rate of increase in the aggregate input, 3.8% was caused by the increase in capital input and 4.8% was caused by the increase in labor input.[22]

---

[22]For this calculation, the following formula was used:

$$I_{kL} = I_k^{.33} \, I_L^{.67}$$

$$G_{I_{kL}} = (.33)\, G_{I_k} + (.67)\, G_{I_L}$$

where .33 and .67 are capital and labor shares, respectively.

TABLE 27

INDICES OF OUTPUT, INDIVIDUAL INPUTS AND AGGREGATE INPUT IN THE NONAGRICULTURAL SECTOR, 1961-1979
(Base year: 1961)

| (1) Year | (2) Output (Value Added) ($I_V$) | (3) Capital ($I_k$) | (4) Labor ($I_L$) | (5) Aggregate Input ($I_{kL}$) |
|---|---|---|---|---|
| 1961 | 1.000 | 1.000 | 1.000 | 1.000 |
| 1962 | 1.075 | 1.054 | 1.084 | 1.075 |
| 1963 | 1.078 | 1.118 | 1.169 | 1.152 |
| 1964 | 1.137 | 1.165 | 1.249 | 1.220 |
| 1965 | 1.348 | 1.236 | 1.408 | 1.346 |
| 1966 | 1.551 | 1.366 | 1.457 | 1.425 |
| 1967 | 1.768 | 1.539 | 1.595 | 1.576 |
| 1968 | 2.005 | 1.788 | 1.758 | 1.768 |
| 1969 | 2.288 | 2.130 | 1.818 | 1.914 |
| 1970 | 2.608 | 2.444 | 1.894 | 2.060 |
| 1971 | 2.873 | 2.762 | 2.074 | 2.269 |
| 1972 | 3.074 | 3.012 | 2.084 | 2.344 |
| 1973 | 3.707 | 3.344 | 2.226 | 2.557 |
| 1974 | 4.120 | 3.672 | 2.399 | 2.792 |
| 1975 | 4.277 | 4.069 | 2.560 | 3.009 |
| 1976 | 4.983 | 4.545 | 2.780 | 3.305 |
| 1977 | 5.502 | 5.123 | 3.007 | 3.600 |
| 1978 | 6.270 | 5.957 | 3.321 | 4.018 |
| 1979 | 7.108 | 6.971 | 3.477 | 4.466 |
| Annual Growth Rate (%) | 11.5 | 11.4 | 7.2 | 8.6 |

SOURCE: Column (2) is calculated from the data of Table 26. Column (3) is calculated from the data of Table 6. Column (4) is calculated from the data of Table 7.

NOTE: Column (5) is calculated from the aggregate input formula: $I_{kL} = I_k^b \times I_L^a$

However, the observed rate of increase in the nonagricultural output (value added) during the same period is 11.5% per annum, as shown in Table 27, column 2. The discrepancy of about 2.9% between the observed and expected rates of increase in nonagricultural income represents the contribution of the total productivity progress broadly defined.

Based upon the aggregate input (index) and output (index) series compiled here, changes in total factor productivity can be calculated by dividing the aggregate input index in Table 27, column 5 into the output index of Table 27, column 2 each year. The results are presented in Table 28, column 2.

Total factor productivity in the nonagricultural sector increased by 60% during the 1961-1979 period at an annual average rate of 2.9%. During the first period (1961-1965), there was no significant change in productivity. Actually, there was a noticeable decline in productivity during the years 1961-1964. The reason was that increased nonagricultural output was brought about mainly by drastic additions to the input factors (capital and labor). Thus, inputs' expansion was the main source of output growth in the first period.

As shown in Table 29, the annual growth rate of total real income was 7.9%. A total of 7.8% of the growth was attributed to the aggregate input growth (capital and labor), while .1% was due to the growth in total productivity. Accordingly, most sources of nonagricultural growth belong to the growth of inputs in this period.

However, improvement in nonagricultural income was considerable in the second period (1965-1970), when total factor productivity impressively increased at an annual rate of 4.9%. During this period,

TABLE 28

INDICES OF FACTOR PRODUCTIVITY IN NONAGRICULTURAL SECTOR, 1961-1979
(Base year: 1961)

| (1)<br>Year | (2)<br>Total Factor Productivity | (3)<br>Capital Productivity | (4)<br>Labor Productivity |
|---|---|---|---|
| 1961 | 1.000 | 1.000 | 1.000 |
| 1962 | 1.000 | 1.020 | 0.992 |
| 1963 | 0.936 | 0.964 | 0.922 |
| 1964 | 0.932 | 0.976 | 0.910 |
| 1965 | 1.001 | 1.091 | 0.957 |
| 1966 | 1.088 | 1.135 | 1.065 |
| 1967 | 1.122 | 1.149 | 1.108 |
| 1968 | 1.134 | 1.121 | 1.141 |
| 1969 | 1.195 | 1.074 | 1.259 |
| 1970 | 1.266 | 1.067 | 1.377 |
| 1971 | 1.266 | 1.040 | 1.385 |
| 1972 | 1.311 | 1.021 | 1.475 |
| 1973 | 1.450 | 1.109 | 1.665 |
| 1974 | 1.476 | 1.122 | 1.717 |
| 1975 | 1.421 | 1.051 | 1.671 |
| 1976 | 1.508 | 1.096 | 1.792 |
| 1977 | 1.528 | 1.074 | 1.830 |
| 1978 | 1.560 | 1.053 | 1.888 |
| 1979 | 1.592 | 1.020 | 2.044 |
| Annual Growth Rate (%) | 2.9 | | |

SOURCE: Data from Table 27.

NOTE: Column (2) is calcualted in the following fashion: $T = I_V/I_{KL}$. Column (3): Capital Productivity = $I_V/I_K$. Column (4): Labor Productivity = $I_V/I_L$.

TABLE 29

EFFECTS OF INPUTS' GROWTH AND PRODUCTIVITY CHANGE ON NONAGRICULTURAL GROWTH, 1961-1979
(Percent)

| (1) Period | (2) Total Income ($G_V$) | (3) Capital ($bG_k$) | (4) Labor ($aG_L$) | (5) Total Productivity ($G_T$) |
|---|---|---|---|---|
| 1961-1965 | 7.9 | 1.8 | 6.0 | 0.1 |
| | (100) | (23) | (76) | (1) |
| 1965-1970 | 14.0 | 5.0 | 4.1 | 4.9 |
| | (100) | (36) | (29) | (35) |
| 1970-1975 | 10.4 | 3.6 | 4.2 | 2.6 |
| | (100) | (35) | (40) | (25) |
| 1975-1979 | 13.5 | 4.9 | 5.3 | 3.2 |
| | (100) | (36) | (39) | (24) |
| 1961-1970 | 11.4 | 3.5 | 5.0 | 2.9 |
| | (100) | (31) | (44) | (25) |
| 1970-1979 | 11.7 | 4.2 | 4.6 | 2.8 |
| | (100) | (36) | (39) | (24) |
| 1961-1979 | 11.5 | 3.8 | 4.8 | 2.9 |
| | (100) | (33) | (42) | (25) |

SOURCE: Data from Table 27 and 28.

NOTE: All figures are calculated according to the growth equation ($G_V = bG_k + aG_L + G_T$), where b and a are capital and labor shares respectively:

1st row $G_V = (.33)\ G_k + (.67)\ G_L + G_T$
2nd row $G_V = (.34)\ G_k + (.66)\ G_L + G_T$
3rd row $G_V = (.33)\ G_k + (.67)\ G_L + G_T$
4th row $G_V = (.34)\ G_k + (.66)\ G_L + G_T$
5th row $G_V = (.33)\ G_k + (.67)\ G_L + G_T$
6th row $G_V = (.34)\ G_k + (.66)\ G_L + G_T$
7th row $G_V = (.335)\ G_k + (.665)\ G_L + G_T$

The figures are average shares of capital and labor for each period.

capital input increased at an average rate of 5.0% and labor input at 4.1% per annum. Thus, an increase in the aggregate input was at an average rate of 9.1% per year. In this connection, the rate of growth in total nonagricultural income was also expected to be 9.1% per annum (if total productivity increased at zero rate). However, the actual growth of nonagricultural income is measured at a rate of 14% (the highest growth rate of the study period). The total factor productivity, the difference (4.9%) between the actual and the expected rate of growth in nonagricultural income contributed highly to the nonagricultural income growth.

During the third period (1970-1975), the rates of expected income growth (aggregate input growth: 7.8%) and productivity improvement (2.6%) decelerated considerably in comparison with those of the former period. As a result, the actual growth rate of nonagricultural income dropped from 14.0% in the second period (1965-1970) to 10.4% in the third period (1970-1975).

During the fourth (last) period, the rate of growth in nonagricultural income increased again to 13.5% per annum. This high growth rate can be attributed to increases in the rates of growth of aggregate input (10.2%) and of the total productivity improvement (3.2%). Thus, about 75% of the growth in nonagricultural income was attributable to aggregate input growth, while the remaining 25% belonged to the contribution of total productivity improvement during the period.

During the 1960s, 31% (3.5 of 11.4%) of 11.4% annual growth in nonagricultural income was attributable to capital growth, while

44% (5.0 of 11.4%) was attributable to the increase in labor force (thus, making 75% attributable to the growth in aggregate input). This left 25% (2.9 of 11.4%) attributable to the total productivity progress.

In the 1970s, Korea's nonagricultural economy experienced a strong capital-deepening tendency ($G_{k/L}$ : 5.5% per annum) in the wake of increases in real wages after the economic turning point, as shown in Figure 5.[23] The growth rate of capital was considerably higher than that of labor during this period. Therefore, capital input contributed to the nonagricultural growth much more in the 1970s than in the 1960s, while total productivity growth slightly dropped from 2.9% per annum in the 1960s to 2.8% in the 1970s. From Table 29, it appears that the relative contribution of the factors was 36% for capital growth, 39% for the labor force growth, and the remaining 24% for the total factor productivity improvement.

So far, sources of growth in nonagricultural income have been traced to increases in three economic factors during each period: capital, labor, and technology (total productivity). Finally, for the entire period (1961-1979), nonagricultural income increased at an average rate of 11.5% per annum. This high growth rate was composed of a capital growth rate of 33%, an increase in labor force of 42%, and a technological improvement of 25%. Combined, the growth in aggregate input (capital and labor) contributed three-fourths of the nonagri-

---

[23]The capital-deepening can be regarded as a growth rate of capital-labor ratio through time (1970-1979):

$$G_{k/L} = G_k - G_L = 12.6 - 7.1 = 5.5\%.$$

cultural income growth, while the productivity improvement accounted for one-fourth of the growth in nonagricultural income.

In this connection, it is interesting to note that capital growth did not play the major role in the contribution to an increase in nonagricultural output, even if capital grew faster than labor in the last two decades. Technological progress was always the lowest contribution to the nonagricultural growth. However, labor input growth has played a more important role in the output growth than any other factors over the entire study period.

Generally speaking, Korea's nonagricultural productivity, which is defined as the ratio of output to input, did not improve significantly, as compared to the increases in physical inputs (capital and labor) during the past two decades. This implies that the physical aggregate input was not utilized effectively--no efficient utilization of machinery, not much improvement in management, and no significant advancement of workers' skill and knowledge.

The physical aggregate input, as shown in Table 27, column 5 and in Figure 7, increased at an average rate of 8.6% per annum during the 1961-1979 period, while the nonphysical input (total productivity) only improved at an annual rate of 2.9% in the same period. Accordingly, the rate of output growth (11.5% per year) certainly resulted from the addition of the physical aggregate input growth rate's 8.6% to the nonphysical productivity improvement's 2.9% as follows:

$$V = T(t)\ f(K,L) \qquad (10)$$

$$\text{Log } V = \text{Log } T + \text{Log } f(K,L)$$

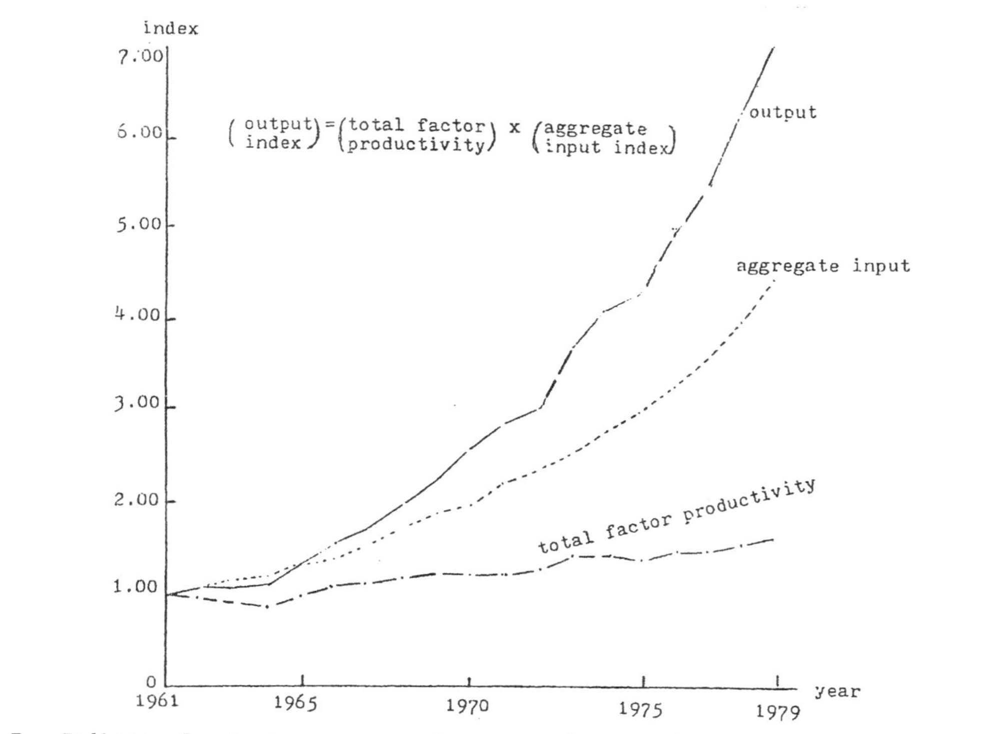


Fig. 7. Indices of output, aggregate input, and total factor productivity (1961-1979). The output index = total factor x aggregate input productivty index.

SOURCE: Data from Tables 27 and 28.

$$G_V = G_T + G_f$$

$$11.5 \quad 2.9 \quad 8.6$$

$$(100\%) \quad (25\%) \quad (75\%)$$

where $G_V$ : output growth rate,

$G_T$ : total productivity growth rate,

and $G_f$ : physical aggregate input growth rate.

According to the above calculation, the physical aggregate input has played a more important role in output growth than the productivity improvement. Three-fourths of the growth in nonagricultural income has been attributed to growth in physical factors and the remaining one-fourth to productivity improvement during the entire period. Thus, the growth of nonagricultural income was almost wholly based on traditional physical inputs (capital and labor) in Korea's nonagricultural economy.

From the previous discussion, it is now apparent by implication that the difference between the increments in output and inputs during the period of 1961-1979 shall be explained in terms of changes in total productivity (technology). Now, one may calculate as follows the unexplained output series that are attributable to the total productivity improvement over time:

$$T_t = V_t - (I_{kL} V_0)_t \tag{11}$$

where $V_t$ : observed total income in the nonagricultural sector each year,

$I_{kL}$: aggregate input index each year (shown in Table 27),

$V_0$ : observed total income in base year,

$(I_{kL}V_0)_t$ : expected income series in the absence of productivity changes each year,

and $T_t$ : unexplained income series due to productivity changes, such as productivity gains.

From Equation 11, the unexpected income series can be measured. The results are presented in Table 30. The appearance of the negative computed unexplained income between 1961 and 1965 seems to be unusual. However, it is possible that the state of the arts in the nonagricultural sector remained very much unchanged or that a situation occurred whereby output was proportionately less than the increased physical inputs (capital and labor) applied--in terms of Ricardo's diminishing returns concept.

Thus, during the first period (1961-1965), total real income produced was not enough to pay for total physical inputs which were utilized in the production, since the diminishing returns took place in the production scale. Table 31 indicates that in the same period, the total average annual physical inputs of 758.77 billion won produced at most the total average annual income of 738.45 billion won by the negative income of 20.32 billion won. This negative income of 20.32 billion won resulted from the same amount of decrease in total productivity gains. Therefore, the share of total physical inputs in total nonagricultural income shows 102.8%, while the remaining negative 2.8% belongs to the share of productivity gains in total real income.

TABLE 30

OBSERVED, EXPECTED AND UNEXPLAINED OUTPUTS, 1961-1979
(Unit: In billion 1970 won)

| (1) Year | (2) Observed Total Real Income $(V_t)$ | (3) Expected Income Owing to Physical Inputs (Total Real Input) $(I_{KL}V_O)_t$ | (4) Unexplained Income Owing to Technological Progress (Productivity Gains) $(T_t)$ |
|---|---|---|---|
| 1961 | 654.90 | 654.90 | 0.00 |
| 1962 | 704.33 | 704.02 | 0.31 |
| 1963 | 705.98 | 754.44 | -48.46 |
| 1964 | 744.35 | 798.98 | -54.63 |
| 1965 | 882.70 | 881.50 | 1.20 |
| 1966 | 1,015.69 | 933.23 | 82.46 |
| 1967 | 1,157.87 | 1,032.12 | 125.75 |
| 1968 | 1,313.09 | 1,157.86 | 155.23 |
| 1969 | 1,498.60 | 1,253.48 | 245.12 |
| 1970 | 1,708.17 | 1,349.09 | 359.08 |
| 1971 | 1,881.31 | 1,485.97 | 395.34 |
| 1972 | 2,012.92 | 1,535.09 | 477.83 |
| 1973 | 2,427.99 | 1,674.58 | 753.41 |
| 1974 | 2,698.41 | 1,828.48 | 869.93 |
| 1975 | 2,800.98 | 1,970.59 | 830.39 |
| 1976 | 3,263.44 | 2,164.44 | 1,099.00 |
| 1977 | 3,603.13 | 2,357.64 | 1,245.49 |
| 1978 | 4,106.47 | 2,631.39 | 1,475.08 |
| 1979 | 4,654.89 | 2,924.78 | 1,730.11 |

SOURCE: Column (2) (Observed Income) is the same as nonagricultural income (v) in Table 26.

NOTE: Column (3) is calculated by $(I_{KL}V_O)_t$ and Column (4) is calculated by $V - (I_{KL}V_O)_t$.

TABLE 31

THE SHARES OF TOTAL PHYSICAL INPUTS AND PRODUCTIVITY GAINS IN NONAGRICULTURAL INCOME, 1961-1979
(Unit: In billion 1970 won)

| (1) Period | (2) Total Physical Inputs per Annum | (3) Total Productivity Gains per Annum | (4) Share of Total Physcial Inputs in Total Income (%) | (5) Share of Total Productivity Gains in Total Income (%) |
|---|---|---|---|---|
| (1st) 1961-1965 | 758.77 | -20.32 | 102.8 | -2.8 |
| (2nd) 1966-1970 | 1,145.16 | 193.53 | 85.5 | 14.5 |
| (3rd) 1971-1975 | 1,698.94 | 665.38 | 71.9 | 28.1 |
| (4th) 1976-1979 | 2,519.56 | 1,387.42 | 64.5 | 35.5 |

SOURCE: Table 30.

During the three periods (1965-1970, 1970-1975, and 1975-1979), the unexplained income (productivity gains), however, increased considerably in addition to the expected income due to physical inputs. The continuous increases in total productivity gains relative to total physical inputs brought about a considerable increase in the share of total productivity gains, from 14.5% in the second period (1965-1970) to 28.1% in the third period (1970-1975), and further to 35.5% in the fourth period (1975-1979).

This may be attributable to the economic scale changes over time. That is to say, below are the following situations:

1. The aggregate production function is not strictly linear--not linearly homogeneous of degree one (technology has changed through time in a strict sense).
2. Quality of factor has changed.
3. General economic efficiency has improved.[24]
4. The degree with which resources are utilized has changed. Thus, if the aggregate production function is not linearly homogeneous, then any deviation from the expected income, due to physical inputs will undoubtedly lead to changes in unexplained income. Whether the aggregate production function is truly homogeneous of degree one and how changes

---

[24]Better transportation facilities, public health conditions, and general institutional frameworks will improve efficiency of non-agricultural output. Although they are important to industrial production, the effects of these variables upon industrial output are not assessable statistically. Therefore, the treatment of the effects of those variables upon the unexplained income is broadly defined as technological progress (total productivity improvement).

in economic scale will affect the nonagricultural output are totally empirical questions.[25]

It will be recalled that we have defined technological neutrality to mean that the upward shifts in the aggregate production function were pure scale changes, leaving marginal rates of substitution untouched at given capital-labor ratios. Over the nineteen year period (1961-1979), the productivity increments (unexplained income growth) resulted from the upward shifts in the aggregate production fucntion, while the growth in output imputed to increases in physical inputs (expected income growth) resulted from the movement along the curve of the production function.[26] Thus, one may separate a change in total observed income between 1961 and 1979 into a change in expected income imputed to physical inputs and productivity incre-

---

[25] In a dynamic sense, the production function implicitly assumed in this section (a linearly homogeneous production function) does not adequately represent the true aggregate production function and is poorly specified because there exists the discrepancy between the observed and expected rates of growth in nonagricultural income (both growth rates are not the same).

[26]

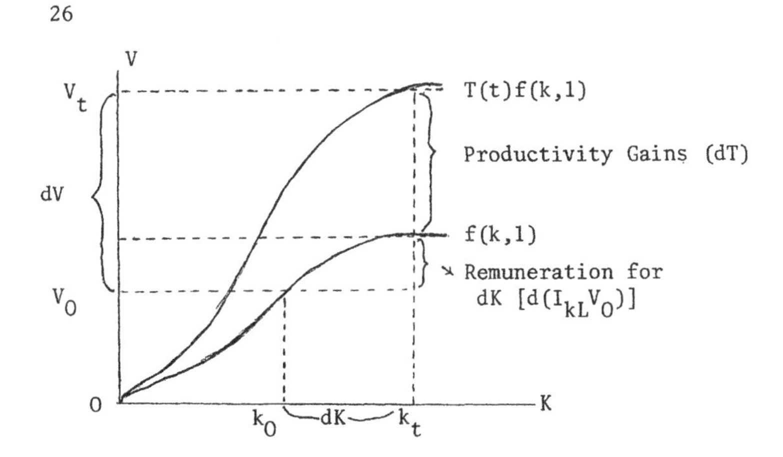

ments (a change in unexplained income) between the two periods. This separation may be seen as follows:

$$V_t - V_0 = [(I_{kL}V_0)_t - (I_{kL}V_0)_0] + (T_t - T_0) \qquad (12)^{27}$$

$$dV = d(I_{kL}V_0) + dT$$

$$d3{,}999.99 = d2{,}269.88 + d1{,}730.11$$

$$(100\%) \qquad (57\%) \qquad (43\%) .$$

As a result of the above calculation, the share of productivity increments of the growth in total observed nonagricultural income is less than that of a change in expected income imputed to physical inputs growth. About 57% of the change in total observed income (3,999.99 billion won) is traceable to growth in physcial inputs and the remaining 43% to productivity improvement.[28]

In summary, sources of the growth in Korea's nonagricultural economy have been attributed to increases in three economic factors; capital, labor, and technology. All these factors have significantly served to improve nonagricultural income during the past two decades.

The highest growth in capital (11.4% per year) did not play a major role in the contribution to an increase in nonagricultural income. However, labor input growth (7.2%) has played a more important role in the total income growth than any other factors. Thus, the

---

[27]Data from Table 30. Unit: billion won.

[28]Professor Solow's study for the American economy during 1919-1949, indicates that productivity improvement accounted for 87.5% of the total output increase and the remaining 12.5% is attributed to the growth in physical inputs. Our study, however, shows that physical inputs formation rather than the productivity improvement is the major contributor to the output growth in Korea's nonagricultural economy.

improperly increasing capital was not utilized effectively in the production process as comparison with labor utilization.

In this connection, technological progress (2.9%) was the lowest contribution to Korea's nonagricultural economic growth. Consequently, the growth in the nonagricultural economy (11.5) has been almost wholly attributed to growth in physical inputs during the period 1961-1979.

## The Effects of Low Productivity Improvements on the Price Level

As mentioned earlier, productivity improvement gives a significant impact on the growth in real product (real income).[29] The real income can change in proportion to changes in total factor productivity in relation to total physical inputs.

An increase in total factor productivity will also raise factor prices (wage and property rates) in relation to the general product price level. Thus, changes in factor prices depend upon changes in total factor productivity in relation to the general product prices. This relationship among the three variables (total factor productivity, total factor price, and general product price) can be derived in terms of the aggregate production function as follows:

$$T = \frac{V}{f(k,L)} \qquad \text{(From Equation 7)}$$

$$T = \frac{V}{f(k,L)} \bigg/ \frac{V^*}{V}$$

[29] The real product and real income are equal in current, as well as in constant won when net output in production is valued at factor cost.

$$T = P_f / P_V \tag{13}$$ [30]

where T : total factor productivity

V* : total product (income) in current price,

V : total income in constant price,

f(k,L) : total factor input (aggregate input) in real terms,

$P_f$ : factor prices (aggregate),

and $P_V$ : product price (general product price level).

Putting the above same equation differently, an increase in general product price ($P_V$) can be explained by means of an increase in total factor price ($P_f$) proportionately greater than the increase in total factor productivity (T) as follows:

$$P_V = P_f/T \tag{14}$$

$$(G_{P_V} = G_{P_f} - G_T).$$

There exists a proportional relationship between the general product price level and total factor price, and an inverse relationship between the general product price and the total productivity improvement. Consequently, increases in aggregate factor prices (wage and property rates) positively affect increases in general product price level--cost-push inflation in macroterms. Productivity improvement, however, can absorb the inflationary shock of an increase in factor prices and thus, can alleviate an increase in general product

---

[30] See John W. Kendrick and Ryuzo Sato, "Factor Prices, Productivity, and Economic Growth," American Economic Review (December 1963), p. 976 (footnote).

price level to a certain degree.

To demonstrate the manner in which the absorption of inflationary shock was made possible by productivity improvement, this section will focus on the comparison between Korea and Taiwan. This effective analysis requires estimates of interrelated variables which Table 32 seeks to provide.

In Table 32, total factor price ($P_f$) is obtained by dividing total current product (income at factor cost) by total real factor input (the sum of real labor and capital inputs). To obtain general product prices ($P_v$), it is necessary to compute the quotient of the total product at factor cost in current prices and in constant prices (base year = 1970). The resulting product price level is nearly the same as the implicit price deflator of national income. Finally, total factor productivity has been defined in the past section as the ratio of real product to the sum of real physical factor inputs in the production function. Thus, the three variables are related precisely as shown in Equations 13 and 14.

For the sake of convenience, Table 33 shows the indices of the three variables based on the year 1970. Over the period 1961-1979, a 20.1% increase in the rate of total factor price necessarily brought about a 17.2% increase in the rate of total product price, which is less than that of the total factor price by 2.9% due to the contribution of productivity improvement. In other words, total productivity improvement absorbed the shock of a 20.1% increase in the rate of factor prices by 2.9% and, therefore, decreased the inflationary impact to 17.2% of the growth in total product price, which was still

TABLE 32

FACTOR PRICES, PRODUCT PRICES AND TOTAL PRODUCTIVITY IN NONAGRICULTURAL ECONOMY, 1961-1979

| (1) | (2) | (3) | (4) | (5) | (6) | (7) |
|---|---|---|---|---|---|---|
| | Total Product (Current) | Total Real Product (1970 won) | Total Factor Input (1970 won) | Total Factor Productivity | Total Factor Prices | General Product Prices |
| Year | (billion won) | | | $[T(t)]$ | $(P_f)$ | $(P_v)$ |
| 1961 | 164.38 | 654.90 | 654.90 | 1.000 | 0.251 | 0.251 |
| 1962 | 201.44 | 704.34 | 704.02 | 1.000 | 0.286 | 0.286 |
| 1963 | 259.80 | 705.98 | 754.44 | 0.936 | 0.344 | 0.368 |
| 1964 | 361.75 | 744.35 | 798.98 | 0.932 | 0.453 | 0.486 |
| 1965 | 464.30 | 882.70 | 881.50 | 1.001 | 0.527 | 0.526 |
| 1966 | 610.43 | 1,015.69 | 933.23 | 1.088 | 0.654 | 0.601 |
| 1967 | 793.14 | 1,157.87 | 1,032.12 | 1.122 | 0.768 | 0.685 |
| 1968 | 1,005.83 | 1,313.09 | 1,157.86 | 1.136 | 0.869 | 0.766 |
| 1969 | 1,299.29 | 1,498.60 | 1,253.48 | 1.195 | 1.037 | 0.867 |
| 1970 | 1,708.17 | 1,708.17 | 1,349.09 | 1.266 | 1.266 | 1.000 |
| 1971 | 2,097.66 | 1,881.31 | 1,485.97 | 1.266 | 1.412 | 1.115 |
| 1972 | 2,570.50 | 2,012.92 | 1,535.09 | 1.311 | 1.674 | 1.277 |
| 1973 | 3,391.90 | 2,427.97 | 1,674.50 | 1.450 | 2.026 | 1.397 |
| 1974 | 4,776.19 | 2,698.41 | 1,828.48 | 1.476 | 2.612 | 1.770 |
| 1975 | 6,159.36 | 2,800.98 | 1,970.59 | 1.421 | 3.126 | 2.199 |
| 1976 | 8,350.45 | 3,263.44 | 2,164.44 | 1.508 | 3.837 | 2.545 |
| 1977 | 10,845.42 | 3,603.13 | 2,357.64 | 1.528 | 4.600 | 3.010 |
| 1978 | 14,910.59 | 4,106.47 | 2,631.39 | 1.560 | 5.666 | 3.631 |
| 1979 | 20,355.83 | 4,654.89 | 2,924.78 | 1.592 | 6.960 | 4.373 |

NOTE: Column (2): Total Current Product is equal to total current income.

Column (3): Total Real Product = total real income based on 1970 won.

Column (4): Total Factor Input is equal to physical aggregate input which is derived as the sum of capital and labor inputs in real terms (see expected income due to physical inputs in Table 30).

Column (5): Data from Table 28, Column (2).

Column (6): Data from Column (2) ÷ Column (4).

Column (7): Data from Column (2) ÷ Column (3).

TABLE 33

INDICES OF AVERAGE AGGREGATE FACTOR PRICES, AVERAGE GENERAL PRODUCT PRICES, AND TOTAL FACTOR PRODUCTIVITY, 1961-1979 (1970 = 1.000)

| (1) Year | (2) Aggregate Factor Price ($P_f$) | (3) General Product Price ($P_v$) | (4) Total Factor Productivity T(t) |
|---|---|---|---|
| 1961 | 0.198 | 0.251 | 0.790 |
| 1962 | 0.226 | 0.286 | 0.790 |
| 1963 | 0.272 | 0.368 | 0.739 |
| 1964 | 0.358 | 0.486 | 0.736 |
| 1965 | 0.416 | 0.526 | 0.791 |
| 1966 | 0.517 | 0.601 | 0.859 |
| 1967 | 0.607 | 0.685 | 0.886 |
| 1968 | 0.686 | 0.766 | 0.897 |
| 1969 | 0.819 | 0.867 | 0.944 |
| 1970 | 1.000 | 1.000 | 1.000 |
| 1971 | 1.115 | 1.115 | 1.000 |
| 1972 | 1.322 | 1.277 | 1.036 |
| 1973 | 1.600 | 1.397 | 1.145 |
| 1974 | 2.063 | 1.770 | 1.166 |
| 1975 | 2.469 | 2.199 | 1.122 |
| 1976 | 3.031 | 2.545 | 1.191 |
| 1977 | 3.633 | 3.010 | 1.207 |
| 1978 | 4.476 | 3.631 | 1.232 |
| 1979 | 5.498 | 4.373 | 1.258 |
| Annual Growth Rate (%) | 20.1 | 17.2 | 2.9 |

SOURCE: Data from Table 32.

NOTE: $T(t) = P_f \div p_V$ and $G_T = Gp_f - Gp_V$. 2.9% = 20.1% - 17.2% data are very highly consistent with the above formula.

highly inflationary in the economy.

Taiwan's nonagricultural economy, however, was maintained by rapid growth and stable prices during the period 1961-1980, although her economy was interrupted by the two oil crises in 1973 and 1979. In Table 34, Taiwan's data show that total factor price, total product price, and total factor productivity increased at an annual rate of 10.0%, 6.9%, and 3.1%, respectively over the period of 1961-1980. A 10.0% annual growth in total factor price was absorbed with a relatively higher productivity improvement of 3.1%. Thus, Taiwan's high productivity improvement contributed to the nullification of the large percentage of inflationary pressure in relation to the relatively low rate of growth in factor price, as compared with that of Korea. Taiwan's productivity improvement then decreased inflationary shock to 6.9% of the increase in total product price, which indicates a fairly stable price level in such a developing economy as in Taiwan.

The contribution of productivity improvement to alleviating inflationary pressure was different between the two countries. This contribution depends upon changes in the two countries' price levels, relative to their productivity improvement through time. As shown in Table 34, Korea experienced considerable inflationary growth in relation to low productivity progress in both the 1960s and the 1970s.

Taiwan, however, was characterized by noninflationary growth with remarkable price stability (3.6% increase per annum) and extremely high productivity improvement (5.1% per year) in the 1960s,

TABLE 34

GROWTH RATES OF PRODUCT PRICE, FACTOR PRICE, AND TOTAL PRODUCTIVITY IN TWO COUNTRIES' NONAGRICULTURAL ECONOMIES
(Percent)

| (1) Country | (2) Period | (3) Growth Rate of Product Price ($G_{P_V}$) | (4) Growth Rate of Factor Price ($G_{P_f}$) | (5) Growth Rate of Total Productivity ($G_T$) | (6) Ratio of Inflation Absorption ($G_T/G_{P_f}$) |
|---|---|---|---|---|---|
| Korean | 1961-1970 | 16.8 | 19.7 | 2.9 | |
| | 1970-1979 | 17.8 | 20.6 | 2.8 | |
| | 1961-1979 | 17.2 | 20.1 | 2.9 | 14.4 |
| Taiwan | 1961-1971 | 3.6 | 8.7 | 5.1 | |
| | 1971-1980 | 10.2 | 11.5 | 1.3 | |
| | 1961-1980 | 6.9 | 10.0 | 3.1 | 31.0 |

SOURCE: Korea's data estimated from Table 33. Taiwan's data adapted from Shirley W. Y. Kuo, The Taiwan Economy in Transition (Boulder: Westview Press, 1983).

NOTE: Column (6) (Ratio of Inflation Absorption) is defined as the ratio of growth rate of total factor productivity to growth rate of total factor price.

and by moderate inflation (10.2%) with low productivity improvement (1.3%) due to the oil crises in the 1970s.

As a result of this comparison, the ratio of Taiwan's inflation-absorption, 31% due to the productivity improvement, became more than twice as large as that of Korea's 14.4% during the entire period. This implies that the strength of Taiwan's productivity improvement effect on alleviating inflationary pressure was more than two times that of Korea's.

It should be noted here that there exists a significant difference between the rates of growth in factor prices of the two countries, as well as a difference in productivity improvements. Over the period of development, Korea's factor prices (wage and capital return) increased much faster than those of Taiwan and that eventually brought about a different product price level in each country.

Based on our development theory in the case of labor surplus economy with limited natural resources, the different growth trends in factor prices are reflected in terms of each country's different intersectoral development pattern between agricultural and nonagricultural sectors.

In the early development period (1950s), Taiwan's economy was oriented from the better preparation of agricultural development via its productivity improvement. Thus, Taiwan's agricultural modernization by the high productivity improvement (3.2% per year) fueled the nonagricultural sector by means of providing agricultural surplus capital, as well as essential sources of food, raw materials, and manpower. The resulting moderate capital growth in Taiwan's nonagricultural sector, which geared to her agricultural modernization in a fine-tuned fashion, maintained a cautious and stable rate of return by the Taiwanese entrepreneurs.[31]

In addition, highly improved agricultural productivity brought about stabilized food prices and the subsequent stabilization of industrial terms of trade in the balanced growth path. These terms of trade continually curbed nonagricultural wage inflation via consumer's preference mechanism between agricultural and nonagricultural goods.[32]

As a result of the moderate increase in capital and the relatively stable wage level due to the balanced growth path, the modest growth in factor price (10.0% per annum) has been achieved, whereas Korea's factor price level was less favorably affected by its unbalanced growth path.

To improve matters, Taiwan's economy, which had previously been based on the outstanding improvement of agricultural productivity also achieved a high productivity improvement (3.1% per year) in the nonagricultural sector during the entire period (1961-1980). This high improvement of nonagricultural productivity absorbed the large percentage of cost-push inflationary shock in relation to the rate of growth in factor prices and, therefore, reduced inflation's impact to 6.9% of growth in product price during the same period.

---

[31]The high (real) interest rate policy maintained by Taiwan's government kept out improper capital growth toward industrialization. Therefore, labor-intensive industrialization was achieved, rather than capital-intensive industrialization.

[32]See footnote 12 of this paper. Also see Fei and Ranis, Labor Surplus Economy, Chapter 5.

Thus, Taiwan managed to moderate factor-cost inflation, due to the balanced growth path, so that Taiwan's economy increased nonagricultural employment substantially through the labor absorption process and achieved labor-intensive industrialization, maintaining a labor-using technological progress in the production technique. Consequently, Taiwan enjoyed an economic prosperity with fair price stability during the past two decades.

Korea's experience, however, has been quite the opposite of Taiwan's development pattern in that Korea deviated from the track of a balanced path. Korea's government attempted to develop the country in a short-cut way by means of a massive drive toward export-oriented and capital-biased industrialization through an open economy from the early period of development.[33] This attempt resulted in agricultural lagging, thus breaking the natural order of the development pattern in the LDCs. The lagging agricultural production via low productivity improvement (1.3% per year) forced a worsening of the terms of trade of the nonagricultural sector in the manner previously analyzed. The resulting worsening of nonagricultural terms of trade inevitably led to industrial wage inflation via consumers' preference forces. Korea's economy experienced this industrial wage inflation, relatively earlier and faster than usual. The wage

---

[33]Since 1961, domestic savings, foreign borrowings, and even monetary expansion have been strictly allocated in monetary forms by the government and massively channeled to the export-industrial sector at a preferential interest rate which was much lower than the rate of inflation. Thus, the export-industrial sector has been beneficially supported in the continuous capital accumulation.

inflation accelerated after the economic turning point, at which time the unlimited supply of labor became exhausted in the traditional sector.

More precisely, the early experienced wage inflation, based on the unbalanced growth path, forced industrial entrepreneurs to substitute capital for labor as labor became relatively more expensive than capital. In this relation, Korea's government mobilized domestic savings, foreign borrowings, and even seigniorage-cum-inflation tax[34] by monetary expansion and then subsidized massive credits of financial resources to the preferred industrial sector at preferential interest rates. Consequently, the rate of return on capital in Korea's nonagricultural industries experienced a highly increasing trend in the case of the low interest rate regime and the high rate of inflation.

Thus, the profit-maximizing entrepreneurs were further induced to substitute capital for labor after the turning point, where the unlimited supply of labor became exhausted in the rural sector. From the theoretical point of view at this point, capital and wage became so closely dependent on each other that every increase in capital directly fed a corresponding increase in wages and/or fed a decrease in the combined technological progress ($B_L + T/E_{LL}$).[35] In turn,

---

[34]Revenue from new money creation. That is, money creation (change in money stock each year) is just the same as revenue from imposing an inflationary tax on the real cash balances held by the general public. For more detailed information, see Robert Mundell, "Growth, Stability, and Inflationary Finance," Journal of Political Economy (April 1965), pp. 97-109.

[35]According to Equation 2, ($G_L + G_w/E_{LL} = G_K + (B_L + T/E_{LL})$, the equation can turn out to be $G_w/E_{LL} = G_k^w + (B_L + T)/E_{LL}$ after the economic turning point at which the unlimited supply of labor became exhausted, that is, $G_L = 0$.

given the combined technological progress, every increase in wage level fueled an additional increase in capital immediately. Such a spiral acceleration was generated, whereby the industrial capital was dramatically and improperly increased at an annual rate of 11.4% and the resulting technological progress (productivity improvement) experienced a relatively slower growth than factor price did.

This unbalanced growth pattern (the improper capital-deepening industrialization, combined with agricultural lagging) necessarily brought about a high growth in factor price (20.1% per annum during the entire period) and a relatively lower growth in total productivity (2.9%) during the entire period (see Table 34 and compare Korea's figures with Taiwan's figures based on the balanced growth path). Thus, the low productivity improvement could not absorb a relatively high growth in factor price enough to alleviate wage-push inflationary pressure. Consequently, Korea experienced high rates of inflation and inflationary economic growth.

On the other hand, Taiwan's economy, which was based on the balanced growth path, experienced a low growth in factor price (10.0% per year) and a relatively high growth in productivity (3.1%). Accordingly, the difference ($G_{P_V}$ = 6.9% : rate of growth in product price level) between the two growths became much smaller than that of Korea's unbalanced growth path, so that Taiwan enjoyed economic prosperity, along with price stability during the development period.

In addition, these two types of growth patterns would have a different impact on the distribution of income in each country. The following chapter will focus on relating the growth pattern to the distribution of income.

CHAPTER IV

# GROWTH AND FUNCTIONAL DISTRIBUTION IN NONAGRICULTURAL SECTOR

This chapter concerns the nature of technolgical progress, shares of productivity gains due to the technological progress, and functional distribution between capital and labor in relation to growth.

During certain periods, the relative shares between factor inputs are no longer constant when the quantities and prices of factor inputs grow at different rates under certain technological conditions in the production process. Thus, it is reasonable to say that the distribution should be explained dynamically in relation to the growth of the economic factors. That is, the relative shares of the factor inputs depend upon changes in factor inputs, factor prices, and the condition of technological progress in the production process through time.

For this analysis, the introduction of constant elasticity of substitution (CES) production function seems to be much more productive and realistic to Korea's experience. The reason is that the general-type of production function may be an adequate approximation and a less restrictive approach that the empirical situation dictates.

The elasticity of substitution between capital and labor in the

CES world is constant, but is not restricted a priori to any value. In this relation, the Cobb-Douglas and Leontief production functions are clearly restrictive and special cases of the CES production function.[36]

In the first section, the theoretical model in relation to the CES production fucntion is presented in order to estimate the nature of technological progress which affects the relative shares of factor inputs. The second section attempts to visualize how the fruits of productivity gains due to the technological progress are distributed to each factor input (capital and labor) through the market forces. Finally, the third section contains an investigation of total nonagricultural income accruing to factor inputs in relation to changes in factor inputs (capital and labor) and changes in factor prices (wage and capital return).

---

[36]The elasticity of substitution ($\sigma$) in the CES function as follows:

$$0 < \sigma < \infty ,$$

the elasticity of substitution in the Cobb-Douglas function:

$$\sigma = 1,$$

the elasticity of substitution in the Leontief function:

$$\sigma = 0,$$

thus, the elasticities of substitution in the Cobb-Douglas and Leontief functions are restricted a priori to one and zero, respectively, whether or not the empirical situation so dictates, regardless of any changes in factor quantities and factor prices over time.

## Nature of Technological Progress in Korea's Nonagricultural Sector

The nature of technological progress may be analyzed on the basis of the CES production function. The CES production function is fitted to time series data covering Korea's nonagricultural sector over the period 1961-1979. This approach reveals the extent of neutral technological progress and the existence of biased technological progress. Thus, the Brown-Cani production function is presented here by:

$$V = Te^{\lambda t}[dK^{-\rho} + (1-d)L^{-\rho}]^{-\frac{m}{\rho}} \qquad (15)$$[37]

where V, K, and L variables are the same as in Equation 7 and the four parameters are $\lambda$, m, d, and $\rho$. Here, these four parameters represent their own specific characteristics of technology. Briefly:

- $\lambda$ is a scale parameter indicating the efficiency of technology.
- m denotes the degree of homogeneity, such as the degree of returns to scale.

---

[37]The CES production function was derived independently by two groups: one consisting of Arrow, Chenery, Minhas, and Solow, and the other of Brown and de Cani. The two derivations are dissimilar: the latter permits any degree of return to scale.

Kenneth J. Arrow, Hollis B. Chenery, B. S. Minhas, and Robert M. Solow, "Capital-Labor Substitution and Economic Efficiency," Review of Economics and Statistics (August 1961), pp. 225-250.

Murray Brown and John S. de Cani, "Technological Change in the United States, 1950-1960," Productivity Measurement Review (May 1962), pp. 26-39, and two papers in Review of Economics and Statistics (November 1962), pp. 402-411 and (November 1963), pp. 386-394.

Idem, "Technological Change and the Distribution of Income," International Economic Review, Vol. 4 (September 1963), pp. 289-309.

d indicates the degree to which the technology is capital intensive.

ρ is the substitution parameter where the elasticity of substitution of capital for labor is defined as:

$$\sigma = 1/(1 + \rho).$$

Now, assume that the CES production function is homogeneous of degree one. That is, m is constrained to unity (constant returns to scale) in the competitive situation, then the production function turns out to be the Arrow, Chenery, Minhas, and Solow (ACMS) function, which is characterized by Hicks' neutral technological progress:[38]

$$V = Te^{\lambda t}[dK^{-\rho} + (1-d)L^{-\rho}]^{-\frac{1}{\rho}} . \tag{16}$$

From some mathematical manipulations of the above equation, the marginal products of labor and capital are, respectively:

$$\frac{\partial V}{\partial L} = Te^{\lambda t} \; (1-d)L^{-\rho-1}[dK^{-\rho}+ (1-d)L^{-\rho}]^{-\frac{1}{\rho} - 1}$$

and $$\frac{\partial V}{\partial K} = Te^{\lambda t} \; dK^{-\rho-1} \; [dK^{-\rho} + (1-d)L^{-\rho}]^{-\frac{1}{\rho} -1}.$$

The marginal rate of substitution of capital and labor (MRS) may be defined as the ratio of marginal products of labor and capital. In competitive assumption, the MRS must equal the real factor price ratio w/r, whereby w is the real wage rate and r is the rate of return on capital:

---

[38]Hicks, Wages, pp. 112-135. The efficiency parameter λ is a scale transformation of inputs into output, but does not affect the marginal rate of substitution. In this case, technological progress is neutral (see above).

$$MRS = \frac{w}{r} = \frac{1-d}{d} \left( \frac{K}{L} \right)^{1 + \rho} \qquad (17)^{39}$$

where the MRS is a function of the ratio of capital to labor. Under the competitive assumption (m = 1 constant return to scale), the efficiency parameter $\lambda$ disappears from the MRS function so that the marginal rate of substitution of capital for labor is independent of that scale parameter $\lambda$. Thus, $\lambda$ stands neutral to both the MRS and the relative shares of capital and labor.

However, there still exist the two nonneutral technological parameters in the MRS function, which do affect the relative shares of the factor inputs, as well as the MRS.[40] They are the capital-intensity parameter d and the substitution parameter $\rho$ in the CES production function. Thus, the MRS and relative shares of labor and capital depend upon changes in those two nonneutral technological parameters in relation to the growth in the ratio of capital and labor

---

[39]From Equation 17, the elasticity of substitution can be derived by taking logarithm in both sides of the equation and then taking partial derivative with respect to MRS (w/r):

$$\frac{\text{Log } (k/L)}{\text{Log } (w/r)} = 1/(1 + \rho) = \sigma.$$

This measures the proportional change in relative factor inputs in repsonse to a proportional change in MRS; that is, the degree of ease with which capital is substituted for labor. $\sigma$ ranges from 0 to $\infty$.

[40]The relative shares of labor and capital can be derived directly by multiplying L/K in both sides of the MRS function as follows:

$$\frac{w}{r}\frac{L}{k} = \frac{1-d}{d} \left(\frac{K}{L}\right)^{-1} \left(\frac{K}{L}\right)^{1 + \rho}$$

$$\frac{w.L}{r.K} = \frac{1-d}{d} \left(\frac{K}{L}\right)^{\rho} = \text{R.S.} \quad \text{(relative share)}.$$

over time.

In other words, changes in the capital intensity and the degree of substitution of capital for labor produce nonneutral technological progress which alter the MRS at each factor input combination. If the MRS is changed such that the marginal product of labor rises relative to that of capital for each combination of capital and labor, there is said to occur a labor-using (capital-saving) technological progress. Labor saving (capital-using) technological progress occurs when the MRS is lowered at every combination of capital and labor.[41] Thus, nonneutral technological progress is produced by changes in the capital intensity of a technology and the elasticity of substitution of capital for labor in relation to growth in factor inputs.

Now, there are three questions to ask:

1. What specific changes in noneutral parameters produce labor or capital saving technological progress?
2. What does labor or capital saving technological progress mean in terms of relative income shares of capital and labor?
3. How can we quantify labor or capital saving technological progress in order to determine the relative income shares between capital and labor?

For the first question, a rise in the capital intensity parameter d clearly brings about a labor-saving (capital-using) direction, since we know that an increase in capital intensity lowers the marginal product of labor relative to that of capital--MRS--according

---

[41]Hicks, Wages, pp. 121-122.

to the MRS function (Equation 17). Therefore, a capital-using (labor-saving) technological progress is produced in all cases when the capital intensity parameter becomes large. In other words, an increase in capital intensity is always labor-saving (capital-using) and a decrease in capital intensity is capital-saving (labor-using).

What happens to the MRS when the substitution parameter is changed? In an economy where capital rises relative to labor, a rise in the elasticity of substitution reduces the marginal product of labor relative to that of capital. Thus, an increase in the elasticity of substitution is labor-saving (capital-using) when capital is growing more rapidly than labor. Alternatively, in an economy where labor is growing faster than capital, a rise in the elasticity of substitution raises the marginal product of labor relative to that of capital. This implies a capital-saving (labor-using) technological progress.

For the second question, it is interesting to know how changes in the capital intensity and the elasticity of substitution, along with the relative movement in capital-labor ratio may affect the distribution of income between capital and labor.[42]

---

[42]We assume a closed economy in this analysis. The reason is because the external economy may affect the relative shares in the internal economy. In the open economy, the introduction of trade affects the relative shares and the distribution of income between capital and labor in each country. According to the H-O-S theory (Heckscher, Ohlin, and Samuelson), trade must decrease (increase) the relative shares in the real or money national income going to the scare (abundant) factor of production. This immediately affects the distribution of income between capital and labor, assuming that the total amounts of the factors of production remains fixed or the factors change in the same proportion.

Concerning this matter, there are two well-known propositions in the neoclassical tradition. The relative income shares are the result of configurations of capital intensity, the elasticity of substitution, and the capital-labor ratio.

The first proposition holds that a factor-saving (a labor-saving) technological progress reduces the relative share of income of that factor (labor) in all cases.[43] The second proposition maintains that if one factor (capital) grows more rapidly than the other (labor), and if the elasticity of substitution is greater than unity, then the relative share of the first factor (capital) increases.[44] Needless to say, if the elasticity of substitution is less than unity, then the relative share of the first factor (capital) decreases. In case the elasticity of substitution is equal to unity (Cobb-Douglas phenomenon), the relative growth in factor will have no effect on the relative shares. From the above propositions, it is clearly known that an increase in the capital intensity is led to a labor-saving (capital-using) direction, which, therefore, increases the capital share relative to the labor share in all cases.

As for a change in the elasticity of substitution, it is observed that a rise in the elasticity of substitution is a labor-saving technological progress if capital is growing more rapidly than labor. This labor-saving direction certainly leads to an increase in the capital share.

Finally, the last question remains to be answered. How can

---

[43]Hicks, Wages, p. 122.

[44]Ibid., p. 117.

we measure a factor-biased technological progress in order to determine the relative shares over time?

From Equation 17, it is readily seen that factor-biased technological progress may be reflected by changes in the capital intensity parameter d through time. By taking the logarithm in both sides of Equation 17, another equation can be written in the following fashion:

$$\log\left(\frac{d}{1-d}\right) = \log\left(\frac{r}{w}\right) + \frac{1}{\sigma}\log\left(\frac{K}{L}\right) \qquad (18)$$[45]

where we can interpret a sustained increase (or decrease) in "d"[46] as indicating a labor-saving (or labor-using) technological progress, which thus implies an increase (decrease) in the capital share relative to the labor share.

In addition to the above model, it is instructive to introduce another statistical model in testing factor-biased technological progress. Suppose the production function is homogeneous of degree one, but is subject to Hicks-biased (Harrod-neutral) technological progress. The CES production function of the Hicks-

---

[45]In Equation 18, d can be determined by the combined forces of two separate factors (wage-rental ratio and capital-labor ratio) and the elasticity of substitution. We know that a rise in $\sigma$ reduces labor share, too, if wages increase relative to the rate of return on capital according to the following equation:

$$wL/rK = (1-d)/d \times (r/w)^{\sigma-1}$$

which is derived from the CES function.

[46]In the ACMS function, d is referred to as the distribution parameter because the relative shares depend on changes in "d" parameter (see Arrow, et al., "Capital-Labor Substitution," p. 230).

neutral technological progress then turns out to be the function of Harrod-neutral (Hicks-biased) technological progress as follows:[47]

$$V = T[dK^{-\rho} + (1-d)\ (e^{\gamma t}L)^{-\rho}]^{-\frac{1}{\rho}}\ . \qquad (19)$$

As we have seen in this form of CES function, it is characterized by labor-augmenting technological progress. In the CES function, whether the Harrod-neutral (Hicks-biased) technological progress is labor-using or not (labor-saving) can be determined according to:

$$-\rho\gamma \gtrless 0. \qquad (20)$$[48]

We are now ready to prepare the statistical model for the estimation of decisive parameters. Thus, through mathematical manipulations,[49] Equation 16 and Equation 19 turn out to be an

---

[47]Robert M. Solow, "Some Recent Development in the Theory of Production," The Theory and Empirical Analysis of Production (NBER, 1967), p. 29 and C. E. Ferguson, "Substitution, Technical Progress, and Returns to Scale," American Economic Review, Vol. 55 (May 1965), p. 299.

[48]Ferguson, "Return to Scale," p. 299.

[49]One may derive Equation 21 from the CES function:

$$V = T[dK^{-\rho} + (1-d)L^{-\rho}]^{-\frac{1}{\rho}}$$

Let $q = V/L$, then we have

$$q = T[d(K/L)^{-\rho} + (1-d)]^{-\frac{1}{\rho}} \qquad (1)$$

Let real wage $w = \partial V/\partial L = T(1-d)\ [d\ (K/L)^{-\rho} + (1-d)]^{-\frac{1}{\rho}-1}$

$$w = q(1-d)\ [d\ (K/L)^{-\rho} + (1-d)]^{-1} \qquad (2)$$

by (1), we have $q^{\rho}T^{-\rho} = [d\ (K/L)^{-\rho} + (1-d)]^{-1}$

identical statistical model because the computational method is the same for Hicks-neutral and Harrod-neutral progress:

$$\log \frac{V}{L} = \frac{1}{1+\rho} \log (1-d) + \frac{1}{1+\rho} \log w + \frac{\rho}{1+\rho} \lambda t \ . \qquad (21)$$

The above statistical equation is linear in the logarithms of average product of labor (V/L) and wage rate (w), and is also linear in t(time-series) as follows:

$$\log (\frac{V}{L})_t = b_0 + b_1 \log w_t + b_2 t + u_t \qquad (22)$$ [50]

where b's are statistical parameters to be estimated by the ordinary least squares method and the decisive parameters can be measured from the b-estimators in the following fashion:

$$\sigma = \frac{1}{1+\rho} = b_1$$

---

put in (2), $q^{1+\rho} = T^{\rho} (1-d)^{-1} w$

by taking log, $\log (q) = \frac{1}{1+\rho} \log [T^{\rho} (1-d)^{-1}] + \frac{1}{1+\rho} \log (w)$

$$\therefore \log (q) = b_0 + b_1 \log (w) \qquad (3)$$

where $b_0 = 1/(1+\rho) \log [T^{\rho} (1-d)^{-1}]$

$b_1 = 1/(1+\rho) = \sigma$ .

Assuming technological progress is Hicks-neutral, then

$$T = e^{\lambda t}$$

$$b_0 = -1/(1+\rho) \log (1-d) + \rho/(1+\rho)\lambda t.$$

Then,

$$\therefore \log (q) = -\frac{1}{1+\rho} \log (1-d) + \frac{1}{1+\rho} \log (w) + \frac{\rho}{1+\rho}\lambda t.$$

[50] Ferguson, "Returns to Scale," p. 299, Equation 11.

$$\lambda = \frac{b_2}{1-b_1}, \text{ and}$$

$$\gamma = \frac{b_2}{1-b_1}$$

where λ and γ are exactly the same result from the quantitative estimation.

This regression model (Equation 22) is fitted to the time-series data (Table 35) of the nonagricultural sector covering the periods 1961-1970, 1970-1979, and 1961-1979. The empirical results from the ordinary least squares estimation are presented below:

1961-1970 $\log (\frac{V}{L})t = .314 + .757 \log w_t + .015t$

t-statistics (12.22) (6.62) (3.18)

$R^2 = .963$

D.W. = 2.06

S.E. = .029

1970-1979 $\log (\frac{V}{L})t = .338 + .898 \log w_t + .0084t$

t-statistics (6.43) (2.80) (.648)

$R^2 = .978$

D.W. = 1.53

S.E. = .023

1961-1979 $\log (\frac{V}{L})t = .316 + .755 \log w_t + .0144t$

t-statistics (15.68) (9.34) (3.87)

$R^2 = .993$

D.W. = 1.87

S.E. = .0245.

According to this statistical interpretation, all the individual

TABLE 35

REAL INCOME, LABOR INPUT, AND REAL WAGE IN NONAGRICULTURAL SECTOR, 1961-1979
(Unit: In 1970 won)

| (1) Year | (2) Real Income (V) Billion Won | (3) Labor Input (L) Billion Won | (4) Real Wage (w) |
|---|---|---|---|
| 1961 | 654.900 | 461.120 | 1.000 |
| 1962 | 704.330 | 499.800 | .972 |
| 1963 | 705.980 | 538.150 | .894 |
| 1964 | 744.350 | 573.990 | .866 |
| 1965 | 882.700 | 643.950 | .899 |
| 1966 | 1,015.690 | 669.470 | .997 |
| 1967 | 1,157.870 | 734.350 | 1.039 |
| 1968 | 1,313.090 | 811.160 | 1.056 |
| 1969 | 1,498.600 | 839.930 | 1.206 |
| 1970 | 1,708.170 | 874.740 | 1.310 |
| 1971 | 1,881.310 | 952.760 | 1.354 |
| 1972 | 2,012.920 | 955.030 | 1.435 |
| 1973 | 2,427.990 | 1,026.480 | 1.558 |
| 1974 | 2,698.410 | 1,112.740 | 1.562 |
| 1975 | 2,800.980 | 1,181.450 | 1.542 |
| 1976 | 3,263.440 | 1,282.980 | 1.649 |
| 1977 | 3,603.130 | 1,373.960 | 1.737 |
| 1978 | 4,106.470 | 1,500.400 | 1.845 |
| 1979 | 4,654.890 | 1,587.370 | 1.877 |

SOURCE: Column (2) nonagricultural real income (V) data from Table 32, Column (3). Column (3) labor input (L) data from Table 38. Column (4) real wage data (w) from Table 38.

NOTE: Labor input is obtained by (index number of labor employed) x (real wage income in base-year 1961).
Real wage (w) is obtained by the quotient of real wage income and labor input each year.

t-statistics are highly significant at the .05 level except the t-variable in the period 1970-1979. Thus, the explanatory variables (log w and t) can strongly explain the dependent variable ($\log \frac{V}{L}$) during all the periods. R-squared ($R^2$), Durbin-Watson statistic (D.W.), and standard errors of regression (S.E.) are very high, close to 2, and very small, respectively, during all the periods. It is, therefore, implied that each dependent variable is highly correlated with the independent variables and the regression model of each period is well-fitted to the data, without significant autocorrelations and with small standard errors of the regression.

After the decisive parameters ($\sigma$, $\lambda$, and $\gamma$) have been estimated, one may compute trends in the d-series (capital intensity) for each year in order to determine the direction of technological progress.

During the entire period (1961-1979), the trends in capital intensity d are measured according to Equation 18 as shown in Table 36. The d-values show period to period fluctuations in short time intervals, but have generally increased from 1961 throughout 1979 as the d-series are shown in Figure 8. This implies that the time series consistently reflected labor-saving technological progress over the past two decades.

During the first period (1961-1965), the d-values substantially increased at an average rate of 3.45% per annum. This indicates that the nonagricultural sector experienced sustained labor-saving technological progress (negative sign), that is, a decrease in the labor share in the first period.

TABLE 36

TRENDS IN CAPITAL INTENSITY (d) AND FACTOR-BIASED TECHNOLOGICAL PROGRESS, 1961-1979

| (1) Period | (2) d | (3) Annual Growth Rate of "d" ($G_d$) | | (4) Direction of Factor-baised Technological Progress ( + : Labor-using) ( - : Labor-saving) | |
|---|---|---|---|---|---|
| (1st) | | | | | |
| 1961 | .241 | | | | |
| 1962 | .252 | | | | |
| 1963 | .242 | | | | |
| 1964 | .268 | | | | |
| 1965 | .275 | 3.45% | | (-) | |
| (2nd) | | | | | |
| 1966 | .278 | | | | |
| 1967 | .279 | | | | |
| 1968 | .286 | | | | |
| 1969 | .276 | | | | |
| 1970 | .277 | -.07% | | (+) | |
| | | | 1.64% | | (-) |
| (3rd) | | | | | |
| 1971 | .275 | | | | |
| 1972 | .285 | | | | |
| 1973 | .309 | | | | |
| 1974 | .324 | | | | |
| 1975 | .320 | 3.92% | | (-) | |
| (4th) | | | | | |
| 1976 | .324 | | | | |
| 1977 | .314 | | | | |
| 1978 | .313 | | | | |
| 1979 | .347 | 2.18% | | (-) | |
| | | | 3.05% | | (-) |

NOTE: Column (2) "d" can be measured according to equation 18 (data from Table 38).

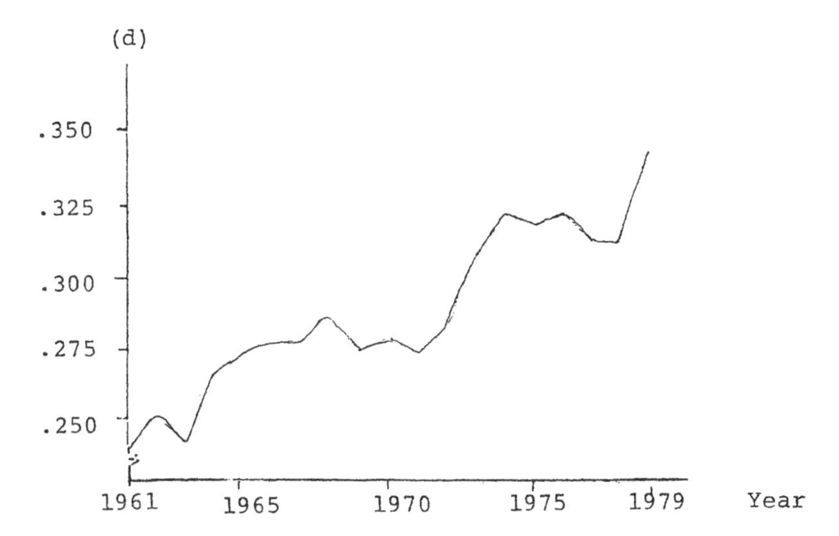


Fig. 8. Trends in capital intensity (d), 1961-1979

SOURCE: "d" data from Table 36.

However, in the second period (1966-1970), the d-series decreased at a rate of .07%, which immediately brought about labor-using technological progress (positive sign), in other words, an improvement in the labor share.

In the third period (1970-1975), the direction of technological progress turned back to a strong labor-saving (3.92% rate of growth in d), and then the labor-saving direction declined a little to a 2.18% rate of growth in d in the fourth period (1975-1979).

Generally speaking, Korea's nonagricultural sector experienced sustained labor-saving technological progress both in the 1960s and in the 1970s. However, the strength of labor-saving progress has been higher in the 1970s (3.05% rate of growth in d) than in the 1960s (1.64%). Consequently, such technological progresses had more unfavorable effects on the labor share in the 1970s than in the 1960s. These functional distribution effects in the nonagricultural sector impacted seriously on the overall household distribution of income as will be seen in the next analysis.

In addition, we still have some significant propositions and another statistical model in determining the direction of technological progress according to the estimated magnitude of decisive parameters as shown in Table 37.

In an economy where capital rises relative to labor, a rise in the elasticity of substitution reduces the marginal product of labor relative to that to capital. Therefore, an increase in the elasticity of substitution leads to labor-saving technological progress (thus, to a decrease in labor share) if capital is growing

TABLE 37

ESTIMATED MAGNITUDE OF DECISIVE PARAMETERS, 1961-1979

| (1) Period | (2) $\sigma$ | (3) $\rho$ | (4) $\lambda$ | (5) $\gamma$ | (6) $-\rho\gamma \gtrless 0$ |
|---|---|---|---|---|---|
| 1960s (1961-1970) | .757 | .321 | .062 | +.062 | -.020 |
| 1970s (1970-1979) | .898 | .114 | .082 | +.082 | -.009 |
| Entire Period (1961-1979) | .755 | .326 | .059 | +.059 | -.019 |

NOTE: Column (3): $\rho = (1/\sigma) - 1$. Column (6): $-\rho\gamma > 0$: Labor-using and $-\rho\gamma < 0$: Labor-saving in terms of Harrodneutral technological progress (Hicks-biased technological progress).

rapidly than labor. It is quite a well-known proposition in the literature of production function.

This is exactly the same situation as Korea's nonagricultural sector for the last two decades. The net fixed capital stock in Korea's nonagricultural sector has grown at an annual rate of 11.4% while the labor force employed in the same sector has increased at an average rate of 7.2% during the period 1961-1979. The elasticity of substitution also increased from .757 in the 1960s to .898 in the 1970s (see Table 37, column 2). In this situation, labor-saving technological progress would be expected and thus also a decrease in the labor share according to the above proposition.

In fact, labor-saving technological progress has been observed and this labor-saving direction actually led to an increase in the capital share between the two periods. Thus, nonneutral technological progress seems to have worsened the labor share in the 1970s more than in the 1960s.

Finally, we are now ready to determine whether Korea's nonagricultural sector experienced Hicks-neutral technological progress or Harrod-neutral (Hicks-biased) technological progress. This is totally an empirical question. According to the Hicks proposition in terms of Hicks-neutral technology progress, an increase in capital is a labor-saving innovation, thus increasing the capital share if its elasticity of substitution is greater than unity. Alternatively, if the elasticity of substitution is less than unity, then an increase in capital relative to labor turns to a labor-using innovation, thus a decrease in the capital share.

Now, concerning Korea's experience, the estimated elasticity of substitution in the entire period (1961-1979) was less than unity, that is, .755, and capital stock grew fast, relative to the labor force employed in the same period. In this case, one would expect an increase in the relative share of labor in Korea's nonagricultural sector. However, this is exactly opposite. Accordingly, there exists an inconsistency between Korea's experience and Hicks proposition, because a labor-saving technological progress (thus, a decrease in the labor share) has actually been observed in Korea's experience.

In order to solve the conflict, however, we now have a choice between Hicks-neutral technological progress and Harrold-neutral (Hicks-biased) technological progress on the basis of the experienced empirical evidence of the decrease in the labor share in Korea's nonagricultural sector. Since a decrease in the labor share has been actually experienced in the first investigation, we assume that it may not fit Hicks-neutral technological progress (Hicks-neutral production function, Equation 16). In other words, the experienced decrease in the labor share can be explained in terms of Harrod-neutral technological progress. It seems reasonable to attribute the decline to labor-saving technological progress in Harrod's neutrality terms. This is shown in Table 37, column 6 based on Equation 20.

All the elasticities of substitution in the 1960s, the 1970s, and for the entire period as a whole were less than unity. In this relation, the capital stock has increased relative to the labor force employed in all the periods. The labor-using technological progresses would then be expected in all the three periods in terms of Hicks' neutrality. However, this is inconsistent with the actual experiences of the decrease in the labor share in all the periods.

The decreases in the labor share in all the periods, however, can be attributed to the labor-saving technological progress in Harrod's neutrality terms. Thus, as shown in Table 37, column 6, the labor-saving technological progresses (negative signs) in terms of Harrod's neutrality took place in the 1960s, the 1970s, and thus, in the entire period. Therefore, Korea's nonagricultural sector experienced decreases in the labor share in the 1960s, the 1970s, and for the entire period.

Now, let us briefly mention the nature of technological progress in Taiwan's industrial economy. In the early period of development, Taiwan's economy started with agricultural modernization through the utilization of multiple cropping agricultural diversification to increase agricultural productivity. This improvement in agricultural productivity played a very important role in fueling the expansion of Taiwan's industrial sector, thus, serving as an essential source of food, raw materials, and agricultural surplus capital for the capital accumulation in the industrial sector.

Furthermore, a significant increase in farm output, resulting from agricultural productivity improvement, led to stabilized agricultural product prices and the subsequent stabilization of industrial terms of trade in the development process. The resulting stable terms of trade between agricultural and industrial goods further stabilized industrial real wage rates via consumer's preference market mechanism. Thus, the stable wage level in the industrial sector stimulated continually the absorption of labor from the rural sector relative to that of capital (see Equation 2).

This situation induced the rapid expansion of labor-intensive light manufacturing goods, due to their relatively simple technologies and their requirement for less capital up until 1970. After 1970, Taiwan's economy gradually shifted from labor-intensive light manufacturing to more capital and skill intensive manufacturing techniques. Therefore, the development of labor-intensive production technique in Taiwan's industrial economy made many meaningful contributions, particularly to the reduction of unemployment and to the improved distribution of income.

In this relation, Mr. Chia-Sheng Wu recently estimated the direction of technological progress in Taiwan's overall manufacturing sector over the two subperiods of 1966-1971 and 1971-1976.[51] His findings, which resulted from his calculation, are that the direction of the technological progress in Taiwan's overall manufacturing sector was labor-using in both periods.

In terms of economic activity, the overall manufacturing sector cannot cover the nonagricultural sector as a whole. However, so far as the overall manufacturing sector includes a large percentage of nonagricultural economic activity, the labor-using technological process in the overall manufacturing sector could roughly represent

---

[51] Chia-Sheng Wu, "Productivity and Wage Structure in Taiwan's Manurfacturing Sector (1966-1979)" (Ph.D. dissertation, University of Utah, 1981), pp. 62-66.

the nature of Taiwan's nonagricultural technological progress.

## Distribution of Productivity Gains Owing to Technological Progress

In the past chapter, we discussed the increase in total real income made possible by productivity improvement. Here, our focus is on the distribution of productivity gains between the two factors: capital and labor.

Productivity gain is the remaining income after the payments of expected income to all the factors which participated in production. In other words, to the extent that actual real income rises more than factor inputs, the difference represents that part of the increase in real income that results from productivity gains. In a certain period, it is possible that the factor inputs are an approximation to what actual real income would have been in the absence of productivity gains.

Thus, productivity gains occurring to factor inputs can be regarded as an unexpected windfall income due to technological progress.[52] These fruits of productivity gains, in addition to the expected income, must be distributed in terms of their factor compensations among all the factors which made contributions to the production.

This section shall investigate the relative factor shares of productivity gains by means of changes in each factor price in relation to total factor productivity ($p_f^*$) change through time. As noted early

---

[52]See Table 30, column 4 and Table 38, all column 4s.

in the previous chapter, productivity gains are the result from increases in total factor price ($p_f$) in nominal terms relative to general product price level ($p_v$).[53] At the same time, the productivity gains are to be distributed more or less to each utilized factor input by means of relative movements in each real factor price. Thus, the shares of the factors in the productivity gains depend on the relative factor price movements in relation to total factor productivity ($p_f^*$: total factor price in real terms).

The conspicuous difference between the increases in real unit earnings of the two factors (real factor prices), relative to the total productivity increase, reflects differential movements in the prices of the two factors (see Figure 9). For instance, a larger increase in real capital price than in total factor productivity can make it possible for real labor price to significantly decrease more or less than the proportionate increase in total factor productivity.

It should be noted that one factor (capital) may appropriate all the total factor productivity gains during a certain period if the real unit income of the other factor (labor) shows no change. Furthermore, in a case where the real wage rate actaully declines in a given period, capital factor can exploit more than the total factor productivity gains. One may notice that Korea's nonagricultural sector experienced this situation in the early 1960s.

For this investigation's purpose, real factor inputs are to be computed on the theoretical base. The real labor input in Table 38

---

[53]See Chapter III, Equation 13.

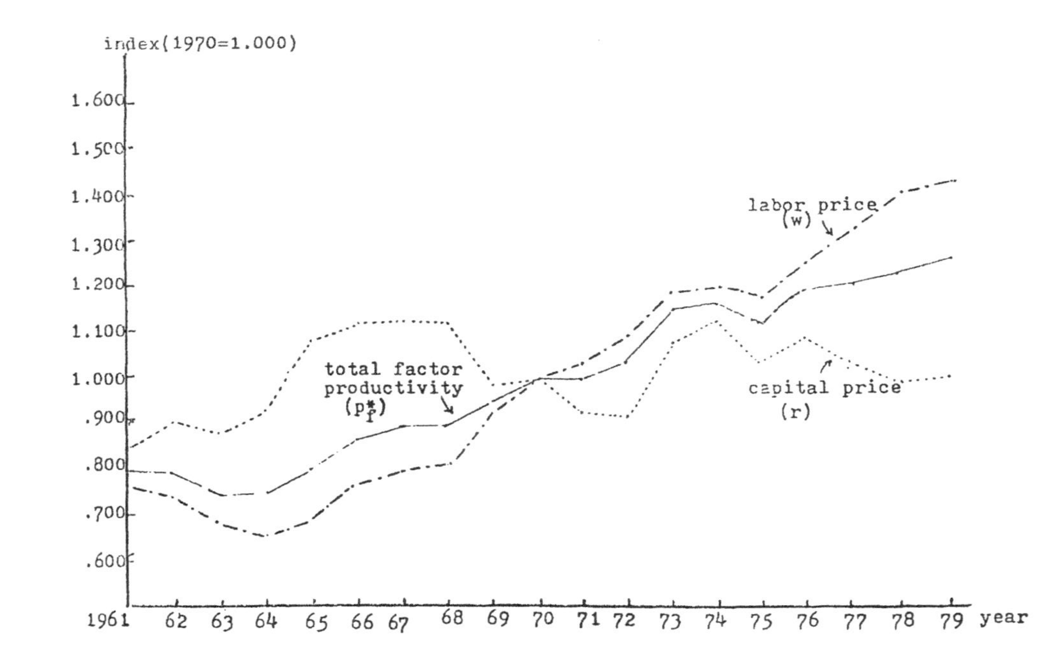


Fig. 9. Trends in real income per unit of factor inputs and total factor productivity (1961-1979).

SOURCE: Table 39.

TABLE 38

FACTOR INPUTS, FACTOR INCOMES AND FACTOR PRODUCTIVITY GAINS
IN NONAGRICULTURAL SECTOR, 1961-1979
(Unit: In billion 1970 won)

| Year | Labor Input | | | | Capital Input | | | | Total Input | | | |
|---|---|---|---|---|---|---|---|---|---|---|---|---|
| | Labor Input | Labor Price | Total Labor Income | Productivity Gains | Capital Input | Capital Price | Total Capital Income | Productivity Gains | Total Input | Total Factor Price | Total Income | Total Productivity Gains |
| | ( L ) | ( w ) | ( wL ) | ( $T_L$ ) | ( K ) | ( r ) | ( rK ) | ( $T_K$ ) | (L+K) | ( $T=p_f^*$ ) | (wL+rK) | ($T_{KL}=T_L+T_K$) |
| | (1) | (2) | (3) | (4) | (1) | (2) | (3) | (4) | (1) | (2) | (3) | (4) |
| 1961 | 461.12 | 1.000 | 461.12 | 0 | 193.78 | 1.000 | 193.78 | 0 | 654.90 | 1.000 | 654.90 | 0 |
| 1962 | 499.80 | .972 | 486.08 | -13.72 | 204.22 | 1.070 | 218.25 | 14.03 | 704.02 | 1.000 | 704.33 | .31 |
| 1963 | 538.15 | .894 | 480.84 | -57.31 | 216.29 | 1.041 | 225.14 | 8.85 | 754.44 | .936 | 705.98 | -48.46 |
| 1964 | 573.99 | .866 | 497.33 | -76.66 | 224.99 | 1.098 | 247.02 | 22.03 | 798.98 | .932 | 744.35 | -54.63 |
| 1965 | 643.95 | .899 | 578.78 | -65.17 | 237.55 | 1.277 | 303.29 | 65.74 | 881.50 | 1.002 | 882.07 | .57 |
| 1966 | 669.47 | .997 | 667.29 | - 2.18 | 263.76 | 1.321 | 348.40 | 84.64 | 933.23 | 1.088 | 1,015.69 | 82.46 |
| 1967 | 734.35 | 1.039 | 762.69 | 28.34 | 297.77 | 1.327 | 395.18 | 97.41 | 1,032.12 | 1.122 | 1,157.87 | 125.75 |
| 1968 | 811.16 | 1.056 | 856.50 | 45.34 | 346.70 | 1.317 | 456.59 | 109.89 | 1,157.86 | 1.134 | 1,313.09 | 155.23 |
| 1969 | 839.93 | 1.206 | 1,013.23 | 173.30 | 413.55 | 1.174 | 485.37 | 71.82 | 1,253.48 | 1.196 | 1,498.60 | 245.12 |
| 1970 | 874.74 | 1.310 | 1,145.77 | 271.03 | 474.35 | 1.186 | 562.40 | 88.05 | 1,349.09 | 1.266 | 1,708.17 | 359.08 |
| 1971 | 952.76 | 1.354 | 1,289.83 | 337.07 | 533.21 | 1.109 | 591.48 | 58.27 | 1,485.97 | 1.266 | 1,881.31 | 395.34 |
| 1972 | 955.03 | 1.435 | 1,370.41 | 415.38 | 580.06 | 1.108 | 642.51 | 62.45 | 1,535.09 | 1.311 | 2,012.92 | 477.83 |
| 1973 | 1,026.48 | 1.558 | 1,599.16 | 572.68 | 648.02 | 1.279 | 828.83 | 180.81 | 1,674.50 | 1.450 | 2,427.99 | 753.49 |
| 1974 | 1,112.74 | 1.562 | 1,738.03 | 625.29 | 715.74 | 1.342 | 960.38 | 244.64 | 1,828.48 | 1.476 | 2,698.41 | 869.93 |
| 1975 | 1,181.45 | 1.542 | 1,822.26 | 640.81 | 789.14 | 1.240 | 978.72 | 189.58 | 1,970.59 | 1.421 | 2,800.98 | 830.39 |
| 1976 | 1,282.98 | 1.649 | 2,115.63 | 832.65 | 881.46 | 1.302 | 1,147.81 | 266.35 | 2,164.44 | 1.508 | 3,263.44 | 1,099.00 |
| 1977 | 1,373.96 | 1.737 | 2,386.10 | 1,012.14 | 983.68 | 1.237 | 1,217.03 | 233.35 | 2,357.64 | 1.528 | 3,603.13 | 1,245.49 |
| 1978 | 1,500.40 | 1.845 | 2,768.93 | 1,268.53 | 1,130.99 | 1.183 | 1,337.54 | 206.55 | 2,631.39 | 1.560 | 4,106.47 | 1,475.08 |
| 1979 | 1,587.37 | 1.877 | 2,979.13 | 1,391.76 | 1,337.41 | 1.253 | 1,675.76 | 338.35 | 2,924.78 | 1.592 | 4,654.89 | 1,730.11 |

SOURCE: Table 45.

NOTE: Factor input is obtained by the product of index number of factor employed and real factor income in the base year 1961.

Real factor price is obtained by the quotient of real factor income and factor input.

Real factor income income (factor compensation) is obtained from Table 45.

Factor productivity gains are obtained by the subtraction of factor input from real factor income. Total factor price ($p_f^*$) in real terms must be equal to total factor productivity (T), since $T = p_f/P_V$, where total nominal factor price ($p_f$) is deflated by general product price level ($p_V$).

is an aggregate of the man-years employed within the nonagricultural sector, weighted by the base-period yearly real labor compensation in each. The real capital input in the same table is also able to be computed by weighting the aggregate of the real capital stock existing in the same sector by the base-period yearly real rate of return on capital in each.[54] This is exactly the same result as the product of index number of yearly factor employed and real factor income in the base-year.

Thus, each real factor input is equal to each factor income in the base-year (1961). The total real factor input is the sum of real labor and capital inputs,[55] and the real incomes of each of the factors add up to total real income at factor cost. Therefore, total real factor input must be equal to total real factor income in the base-year (1961).

Each individual factor price and the total composite factor price ($p_f^*$) in real terms are able to be computed by the quotient of each real income and each real input. Finally, since we quantified each real factor input weighted by the base-year product, each factor's productivity gain is ready to be obtained by the substraction of each factor input from each factor income. Here, the individual factor productivity gains must add up to total factor productivity gains as shown in Table 38.

---

[54]Kendrick, et al., "Factor Prices," Appendix B, p. 1001.

[55]Total real factor input can be derived differently by the product of aggregate input index ($I_{kL}$) and total real factor income ($V_0$) in the base-year, 1961, as shown in Table 30. The result is exactly the same.

Table 38 helps us to analyze the movements in relative factor prices, such as relative changes in real income per unit of labor and capital inputs in relation to total factor productivity that is the same as total composite factor price ($p_f^*$) in real terms.[56]

Table 39 and Figure 9 clearly indicate the movements in real factor prices in relation to total factor productivity. It generally follows that real factor prices do increase in proportion to changes in total factor productivity over the entire period (1961-1979). The difference between the increases in real unit earnings of the two factors relative to the total factor productivity increase reflects the differential movements in the real prices of the two factors. If the increase in real price of capital exceeds total factor productivity increase, this discrepancy must be offset by an opposite divergence between the real price of labor and total factor productivity.

Over the entire period (1961-1979), an increase in real labor price (w) of 3.6% per year exceeded the increase in total factor productivity ($p_f^*$) of 2.9% per year by .7%. This excess must be offset by the fact that an increase in real capital price (r) of 1.3% was outstripped by the increase in total factor productivity of 2.9% by 1.6%.

It should be noted that during the first period (1961-1965)

---

[56]Total factor productivity is, theoretically, the same as total factor price ($p_f^*$) in real terms, since $T = p_f/p_v$ where $p_f$ (total factor price in nominal terms) is deflated by $p_v$ (general product price level) and turns out to be T.

TABLE 39

INDICES OF REAL FACTOR PRICE AND TOTAL FACTOR PRODUCTIVITY, 1961-1979 (1970 = 1.000)

| (1) Year | (2) Real Labor Price (w) | (3) Real Capital Price (r) | (4) Total Factor Productivity ($T = p_f^*$) |
|---|---|---|---|
| 1961 | .763 | .843 | .790 |
| 1962 | .741 | .902 | .790 |
| 1963 | .682 | .878 | .739 |
| 1964 | .661 | .926 | .736 |
| 1965 | .686 | 1.078 | .791 |
| 1966 | .760 | 1.113 | .859 |
| 1967 | .793 | 1.118 | .886 |
| 1968 | .807 | 1.111 | .897 |
| 1969 | .920 | .990 | .944 |
| 1970 | 1.000 | 1.000 | 1.000 |
| 1971 | 1.033 | .935 | 1.000 |
| 1972 | 1.095 | .933 | 1.036 |
| 1973 | 1.189 | 1.079 | 1.145 |
| 1974 | 1.193 | 1.132 | 1.166 |
| 1975 | 1.177 | 1.045 | 1.122 |
| 1976 | 1.259 | 1.098 | 1.191 |
| 1977 | 1.326 | 1.043 | 1.207 |
| 1978 | 1.409 | .997 | 1.232 |
| 1979 | 1.433 | 1.056 | 1.258 |
| Annual Growth Rate | 3.6 | 1.3 | 2.9 |

SOURCE: Table 38.

NOTE: Total factor productivity is equal to total factor price in real terms ($p_f^*$).

real labor price (w) decreased at an average annual rate of 2.7% and real capital price (r) increased at an average rate of 6.7% in relation to a .2% slight increase in total factor productivity ($p_f^*$). Accordingly, capital appropriated more than the total productivity gains, since the real labor price actually declined no matter what relative factor inputs increased in this period. All the productivity gains accrued to capital and even some part of labor income, due to the labor input, were exploited by capital (see Table 40, 1st row).

As a result of a decline in real labor price in this period, the productivity gains accruing to labor became -212.86 billion won which were totally a portion of labor income not due to productivity improvement but due to the real labor input that participated in the production. This amount of labor income was transferred by the market forces to the productivity gains of 110.65 billion won accruing to capital and to the total factor productivity gains of 102.21 billion won.

However, during all three periods (1965-1970, 1970-1975, and 1975-1979), a remarkable increase in real labor price (w) of 5.5% per annum after the economic turning point exceeded the increase in total factor productivity of 3.4% per year. On the other hand, real capital price (r) slightly increased at an annual rate of .05% as compared with a 3.4% of total factor productivity increase. Thus, the market forces of both positive increasing rates of each real factor price averted a conflict on the exploitation of real income due to each real factor input. Workers and entrepreneurs, however,

TABLE 40

FACTOR SHARES IN PRODUCTIVITY GAINS, 1961-1979
(Unit: In billion 1970 won)

| (1) Period | (2) Productivity Gains Accruing to Labor | (3) Productivity Gains Accruing to Capital | (4) Total Productivity Gains | (5) Labor Share in Productivity Gains (%) | (6) Capital Share in Productivity Gains (%) |
|---|---|---|---|---|---|
| (1st) (1961-1965) | -212.86 (-42.57) | +110.65 (+22.13) | -102.21 (-20.44) | Being Appropriated | Having Appropriated |
| (2nd) (1966-1970) | 515.83 (103.17) | 451.81 (90.36) | 967.64 (193.53) | 53.3 | 46.7 |
| (3rd) (1971-1975) | 2,591.23 (518.25) | 735.75 (147.15) | 3,326.98 (665.40) | 77.9 | 22.1 |
| (4th) (1976-1979) | 4,505.08 (1,126.27) | 1,044.60 (261.15) | 5,549.68 (1,387.42) | 81.2 | 18.8 |

SOURCE: Productivity gains computed from estimates shown in Table 38.

NOTE: Figures in parenthesis are average productivity gains per annum.

still struggled for unexpected windfall income due to technological progress, that is, productivity gains.

As mentioned earlier in this section, the relative shares of productivity gains depend on the relative real factor price movements in relation to total factor productivity, regardless of any changes in relative factor inputs. Therefore, the lack of considerable movement in real capital price over the period 1965-1979 implies that most productivity gains actually accrued to labor. The labor share in productivity gains increased from 53.3% in the second period to 77.9% in the third period and further to 81.2% in the fourth period. Thus, as compared with capital, labor has obtained a large proportion of the productivity gains in a static sense.

In a dynamic sense, the estimates in Table 38 allow us to measure the factor share of the productivity increments as shown in Table 41. The real income increments resulting from productivity improvement between two periods can be estimated as the difference between the change in real income and the change in real factor input.

In the presence of productivity improvement during each period, the change in real income is always greater than the change in real factor input so that there exists the positive difference between the two changes; that is, productivity increments between the two periods. In the presence of productivity retrogression, the change in real income is always less than the change in real factor input so that there exists the negative difference between the two changes. That is, productivity decrements between the two periods.

TABLE 41

FACTOR SHARES IN PRODUCTIVITY INCREMENTS, 1961-1979
(Unit: In billion 1970 won)

| | 1961-1965 | 1965-1970 | 1970-1975 | 1975-1979 | 1961-1979 |
|---|---|---|---|---|---|
| Total | | | | | |
| Change in real income (product) | 227.17 | 828.10 | 1,092.81 | 1,853.91 | 3,999.99 |
| Change in factor input | 226.60 | 467.59 | 621.50 | 954.19 | 2,269.88 |
| Productivity increments [(1) - (2)] | .57 | 358.51 | 471.31 | 899.72 | 1,730.11 |
| Labor | | | | | |
| Change in real income (product) | 117.66 | 566.99 | 676.49 | 1,156.87 | 2,518.01 |
| Change in input | 182.83 | 230.79 | 306.71 | 405.92 | 1,126.25 |
| Labor's productivity increments (1-2) | -65.17 | 336.20 | 369.78 | 750.95 | 1,391.76 |
| Labor share of total productivity increments | -114.3 % | 93.8 % | 78.5 % | 83.5 % | 80.4 % |
| Capital | | | | | |
| Change in real income (product) | 109.51 | 259.11 | 416.32 | 697.04 | 1,481.98 |
| Change in input | 43.77 | 236.80 | 314.79 | 548.27 | 1,143.63 |
| Capital's productivity increments (1-2) | 65.74 | 22.31 | 101.53 | 148.77 | 338.35 |
| Capital share of total productivity increments | +214.3 % | 6.2 % | 21.5 % | 16.5 % | 19.6 % |

SOURCE: Changes in real income and input computed from estimates shown in Table 38.

In the absence of productivity improvement in each period the change in real income is equal to the change in real factor input so that there exists no difference between the two changes, that is, no productivity increments between two periods.[57] This proposition holds equally true for total, labor, and capital factors, respectively.

During the period 1961-1965, the changes in each real income of labor and capital add up to the change in total real income of 227.17 billion won. In the same fashion, the changes in each real input of labor and capital add up to the change in total factor input of 226.60 billion won. The excess of change in total real income (227.17 billion won) over the change in total factor input (226.17 billion won) adds up to the total productivity increments of .57 billion won.

Now, there exists a question of how the market forces distribute the total factor productivity increments of .57 billion won to the two factors in the case that the real labor price actually declined in relation to an increase in total factor productivity.

In the labor sector of Table 41, the change in real income (117.66 billion won) was less than the change in real labor input (182.83 billion won). Therefore, there exists the negative difference of 65.17 billion won between the two changes, which is labor's

---

[57] John W. Kendrick, Productivity Trends in the United States (Princeton: Princeton University Press, 1961), p. 129.

productivity decrements.

However, in the capital sector during the same period, the change in real capital income (109.51 billion won) exceeds the change in real capital input (43.77 billion won), so that the positive difference brought about a 65.74 billion won productivity increment accruing to capital.

In these circumstances, capital appropriated more than all the total productivity increment. Capital apparently exploited not only the total productivity increments of .57 billion won, but also the real labor income of 65.17 billion due to the real labor input. This adds up to a 65.74 billion won productivity increment accruing to capital in this period (1961-1965).

In the same fashion, the relative shares in total productivity increments of the remaining three periods (1965-1970, 1970-1975, and 1975-1979) may be traced, as shown in Table 41. In each period after the first period, the excess of change in total real income over the change in total factor input resulted in large positive total productivity increments due to technoloigcal progress. The distribution of the large amount of productivity increments in each period depended on the relative movements in real factor prices in relation to total factor productivity ($p_f^*$) as shown in Figure 9. Thus, the change in each real factor income exceeded the change in each real factor input during all the three periods so that each factor gained more or less the fruits of total productivity increments without any exploitation of its own income of factor input.

The labor shares in productivity increments became generally high as compared with the capital shares; 93.8% in the second period, 78.5% in the third period, and 83.5% in the fourth period.

Generally speaking, the lack of considerable movements in real capital price and the drastic increase in real wages, in relation to a steady growth in total factor productivity, brought about a higher percentage of labor share (80.4%) than of capital share (19.6%) in the total productivity increments during the entire period 1961-1979.

## Functional Distribution of Nonagricultural Income

We have seen the nature of labor-saving (capital-using) technological progress in Korea's nonagricultural sector earlier in this chapter. This labor-saving direction of technological progress was said to reduce the relative share of labor income (Hicks' first proposition). Therefore, a worsening of labor share may be expected in analyzing the functional distribution of Korea's nonagricultural income.

In the second section of this chapter, the distribution of productivity gains has been examined in terms of relative movements in each price of factor inputs in relation to total factor productivity changes, regardless of any change in factor inputs. As a result, the productivity gains have been distributed highly in favor of workers, both in static and in dynamic analyses, except for the period of 1961-1965.

Now, our focus in this section is on the functional distribution of Korea's nonagricultural income as a whole. For this analysis, the change in the income shares of the factors can be quantified in two alternative ways.

The trends in the real prices of the factors and in the quantities of factor inputs employed are of interest as determinants of changes in the real incomes of the owners of the factors. In the course of economic growth, changes in the relative prices of labor and capital and in the relative quantities of the factor inputs can determine the changes in the functional distribution of the whole income and also influence overall distribution of income.

One approach to functional distribution is to quantify changes in income shares as the product of changes in the relative real prices of the factors and in the relative quantities of factor inputs. This equation is presented as follows:

$$\frac{W}{R} = \frac{w}{r} \times \frac{L}{K} = \frac{w}{r} / \frac{K}{L} \qquad (23)$$[58]

where W : aggregate wage compensation,

R : total property income,

W/R : relative income share,

w : real wage per labor input,

r : real rate of return on capital,

L : labor input in real terms,

and K : capital input in real terms.

---

[58] Irving B. Kravis, "Relative Income Shares in Fact and Theory," American Economic Review, Vol. 49 (December 1959).

According to Equation 23, the relative shares of labor and capital result from the product (quotient) of wage-rental ratio and labor-capital ratio (capital-labor ratio). Therefore, the rates of changes in the relative labor shares will vary in accordance to the net effect of the rates of changes in the price ratio and in the quantity ratio. Then, Equation 23 becomes, in a dynamic sense:

$$G_{W/R} = G_{w/r} - G_{k/L} \tag{24}$$

where G stands for growth in the subscripts.

In the historical data of Korea's nonagricultural economy, the price and quantity ratios (w/r and k/L) did move in opposite directions. This implies the factor substitution which served as a built-in stabilizing mechanism, limiting changes in relative shares. Table 42 shows that growths in the relative factor price ($G_{w/r}$) and in the relative factor input ($G_{k/L}$) add up to the net effect of growth in the relative labor share ($G_{W/R}$).

In the first period, the decrease in wage-rental ratio exceeded the decrease in capital-labor ratio, so that their net effect on growth in the relative labor share indicates a -5.21%. The tendency of a decrease in the ratio of capital to labor was not strong enough to offset the relative price change. As a result, the relative share of wage income (W/R) decreased at an average rate of 5.21% per annum in the first period.

In the second period, however, the situation was completely reversed. The real wage increased drastically after the economic turning point relative to real capital return, so that a 9.81% high

TABLE 42

GROWTH IN RELATIVE SHARE OF LABOR IN NONAGRICULTURAL INCOME, 1961-1979
(Percent)

| (1) Period | (2) Growth in w/r ($G_{w/r}$) | (3) Growth in K/L ($G_{K/L}$) | (4) Growth in Wage Income/Property Income ($G_{W/R}$) |
|---|---|---|---|
| (1st) (1961-1965) | -8.38 | -3.17 | -5.21 |
| (2nd) (1965-1970) | 9.81 | 8.08 | +1.73 |
| (3rd) (1970-1975) | 2.61 | 4.29 | -1.68 |
| (4th) (1975-1979) | 4.95 | 6.04 | -1.09 |
| 1960s (1961-1970) | 1.72 | 3.08 | -1.36 |
| 1970s (1971-1979) | 3.65 | 5.07 | -1.42 |

SOURCE: Table 38.

NOTE: W/R = (wage income/property income). $W/R = wL/rK = (w/r)/(K/L)$. $G_{W/R} = G_{w/r} - G_{K/L}$. Column (4) +: an increase in labor share. Column (4) -: a decrease in labor share.

growth rate of wage-rental ratio exceeded a 8.08% growth rate of capital-labor ratio by +1.73%. This indicates that the relative share of labor income increased at an annual rate of 1.73% in the second period.

It is only in the second period that a positive increase in the relative share of labor income took place in Korea's nonagricultural sector. That is consistent with the period in which there did exist the labor-using technological progress, as shown previously in Table 36, column 4.

During the third and fourth periods, a more rapid increase in capital than in labor inputs made it possible for the growth in capital-labor ratio to exceed the growth rate of the wage-rental ratio. Thus, the differences between growth rates in wage-rental ratio and in capital-labor ratio indicate negative growth rates of the relative share of labor income, that is, -1.68% in the third period and -1.09% in the fourth period.

The relative shares of labor income also decreased at an average rate of 1.36% in the 1960s and of 1.42% per annum in the 1970s. However, the relative share of labor income was worse in the 1970s than in the 1960s.

The second approach to the functional distribution is to clearly visualize the movements in the relative shares of the factors by means of a table and figure in the static sense. As noted earlier in this section, the total income accruing to each factor is the product of the input quantity employed and its real price. Aggregate nonagricultural income is the sum of the compensations of all the factor inputs. Accordingly, the relative shares of each factor in the total nonagricultural income depend on the product of the input quantity of each factor relative to the total factor input and the real price of each factor input relative to the total real factor price ($p_f^*$). This equation may be expressed as follows:

$$\left(\frac{W}{W+R}\right)_t = \left(\frac{L}{L+k}\right)_t \left(\frac{w}{p_f}\right)_t \qquad (25)$$

$$\left[\text{or } \left(\frac{R}{W+R}\right)_t = \left(\frac{K}{L+K}\right)_t \left(\frac{r}{p_f^*}\right)_t\right]$$

where all the variables except for $p_f^*$ are the same as those of Equation 23. One additional variable $p_f^*$ is the total factor price in real terms, which is equal to the total factor productivity as shown in Table 38.

Equation 25 indicates that the share of labor income in each year is the product of the labor input share of the total factor input and the labor price share of the total factor price. The share of capital income can be calculated in the same way. Thus, the time-series functional distribution of Korea's nonagricultural income results from such calculations as shown in Table 43, columns 6 and 7.

It is clearly seen from Table 43, column 6, that the labor share in Korea's nonagricultural income generally declined in the entire study period of 1961-1979. The results can be traceable to the movements in each factor input share [L/(L+k) or K/(L+k)] and in each factor price share ($w/p_f^*$ or $r/p_f^*$). It should be noted that the factor input

TABLE 43

DISTRIBUTION OF NONAGRICULTURAL INCOME IN RELATION TO CHANGES IN RELATIVE FACTOR INPUT AND CHANGES IN RELATIVE FACTOR PRICE, 1961-1979

| | Relative Real Factor Input | | Relative Real Factor Price | | Distribution of Nonagricultural Income | |
|---|---|---|---|---|---|---|
| Year | Labor (L/L+k) | Capital (k/L+k) | Labor ($w/p_f^*$) | Capital ($r/p_f^*$) | Labor (2)x(4) | Capital (3)x(5) |
| (1) | (2) | (3) | (4) | (5) | (6) | (7) |
| 1961 | .704 | .296 | 1.000 | 1.000 | .704 | .296 |
| 1962 | .710 | .290 | .972 | 1.070 | .690 | .310 |
| 1963 | .713 | .287 | .955 | 1.112 | .681 | .319 |
| 1964 | .718 | .282 | .929 | 1.178 | .668 | .332 |
| 1965 | .731 | .269 | .897 | 1.274 | .656 | .344 |
| 1966 | .717 | .283 | .916 | 1.214 | .657 | .343 |
| 1967 | .711 | .289 | .926 | 1.183 | .658 | .342 |
| 1968 | .701 | .299 | .931 | 1.161 | .652 | .348 |
| 1969 | .670 | .330 | 1.008 | .982 | .676 | .324 |
| 1970 | .648 | .352 | 1.035 | .937 | .671 | .329 |
| 1971 | .641 | .359 | 1.070 | .876 | .686 | .314 |
| 1972 | .622 | .378 | 1.095 | .845 | .681 | .319 |
| 1973 | .613 | .387 | 1.074 | .882 | .659 | .341 |
| 1974 | .609 | .391 | 1.058 | .909 | .644 | .356 |
| 1975 | .600 | .400 | 1.085 | .873 | .651 | .349 |
| 1976 | .593 | .407 | 1.094 | .863 | .648 | .352 |
| 1977 | .583 | .417 | 1.136 | .810 | .662 | .338 |
| 1978 | .570 | .430 | 1.183 | .758 | .674 | .326 |
| 1979 | .543 | .457 | 1.179 | .787 | .640 | .360 |

SOURCE: Table 38.

NOTE: Column (2) Ratio of labor input to total factor input.
Column (3) Ratio of capital input to total factor input.
Column (4) Ratio of real wage rate total factor price.
Column (5) Ratio of real capital return to total factor price.
Column (6) Product of relative labor input and relative real wage rate.
Column (7) Product of relative capital input and relative real capital return.

shares of labor and of capital moved in opposite directions, as did the factor price shares of labor and of capital. The factor input share and its corresponding factor price share also moved inversely, due to the factor substitution.

In this connection, the labor input share declined from 70.4% in 1961 to 64.8% in 1970 and further to 54.3% in 1979. The decline in the labor input share was associated with a less than proportional increase in the labor price share. From 1961 to 1970, the labor input share decreased by 8.0%, while the corresponding labor price share increased by 3.5% (even if declined by 6.9% in the subperiod, 1961-1968). The net effect on the labor share of these inverse movements of the labor input share to the labor price share obviously resulted in a decrease in the labor share from 70.4% in 1961 to 67.1% in 1970.

From 1970 to 1979, the labor input share further decreased by 16.2%, while the labor price share increased by 13.9%. The decline in the labor input share was much larger than the increase in the labor price share, so that the labor share in Korea's nonagricultural income decreased continually from 67.1% in 1970 to 64% in 1979.

During the first period, 1961-1965, the labor input share increased by 3.8%, while the labor price share declined by 10.3%. Thus, the decline in the labor price share was more than the increase in the labor input share. The net effect on the labor share of the inverse movements in the labor input share to the labor price share caused a decrease in the labor share from 70.4% in 1961 to 65.6% in 1965.

However, in the second period of 1965-1970, the labor share of income increased from 65.6% in 1965 to 67.1% in 1970. That is precisely consistent with the previous analyses. The result came from the positive net effect on the labor share of a 15.4% increase in the labor price share, less a 11.4% decline in the labor input share from 1965 to 1970.

From 1970 through 1979, the labor share declined again. The reason is that an improper increase in capital input relative to labor input exceeded an increase in labor price relative to capital price in the course of the substitution of capital for labor after the economic turning point. Accordingly, during both periods, 1970-1975 and 1975-1979, the drastic increases in the capital input share were significantly larger than the declines in the capital price share. As a result, the capital shares in both periods increased from 32.9% in 1970 to 34.9% in 1975 and from 34.9% in 1975 to 36% in 1979.

The functional distribution of nonagricultural income can be visualized in Figure 10. The labor share of income was greater in the 1960s than in the 1970s, due to the fact that the labor share increased by 2.3% only in the subperiod of 1965-1970.

In summary, the labor share of Korea's nonagricultural income diminished in the course of the substitution of capital and labor by changes in factor prices, due to the market forces. In more technical terms, the significant worsening of the labor share of income can be traced to the pattern of capital-intensive industrial growth, namely, a labor-saving technological progress in the nonagricultural economy.

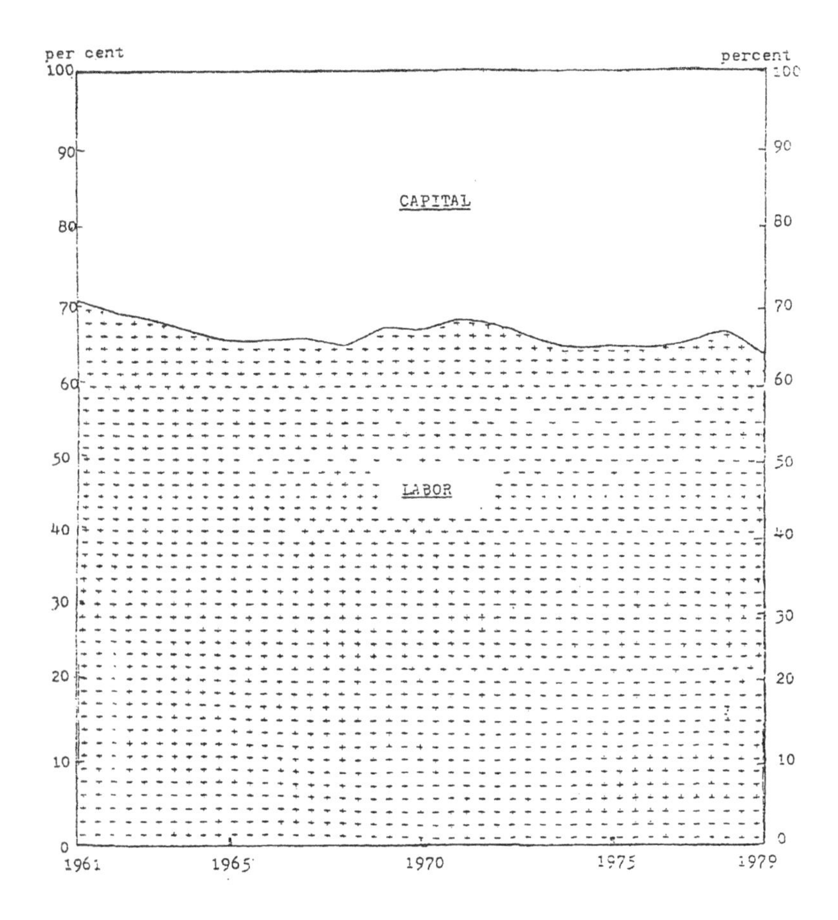


Fig. 10. Factor shares of nonagricultural income (1961-1979).

SOURCE: Table 43.

The improper capital-deepening industrial growth, which experienced high wage inflation due to the inadequate agricultural participation, served to worsen not only the functional distribution of nonagricultural income, but also the overall distribution of national income.

In comparison, however, Taiwan's nonagricultural economy was quite different from that of Korea. The pattern of the relative share of labor income in Taiwan's nonagricultural sector shows a steady improvement in both the 1960s and the 1970s. The labor share improved continually from 64% in 1946 to 68% in 1970, and further improved to 71% in 1978, as shown in Table 44.

This increase of the labor share in Taiwan's nonagricultural income can be attributed to the growth pattern of labor-intensive industrialization which was rooted in the agricultural modernization from the early stage of development. The improvement in agricultural productivity through utilization of multiple cropping and agricultural diversification palyed an important role in fueling the expansion of Taiwan's nonfarm economy. The steady flow of agricultural surplus from an increase in farm output was properly channelized toward the capital formation in the industrial sector. Thus, the industrial capital growth has been harmonized with agricultural development, which led to an increase in agricultural productivity. The subsequent stabilization of industrial terms of trade stabilized industrial real wages in terms of industrial goods. Consequently, the stable wage level in the industrial sector continually stimulated the absorption of labor relative to capital. This adoption of a

TABLE 44

FUNCTIONAL DISTRIBUTIVE SHARE OF NONAGRICULTURAL INCOME IN TAIWAN, 1964-1978
(Percent)

| (1) Period | (2) Labor Share | (3) Capital Share | (4) Total |
|---|---|---|---|
| 1964 | 64 | 36 | 100 |
| 1966 | 65 | 35 | 100 |
| 1968 | 65 | 35 | 100 |
| 1970 | 68 | 32 | 100 |
| 1972 | 70 | 30 | 100 |
| 1974 | 71 | 29 | 100 |
| 1976 | 70 | 30 | 100 |
| 1978 | 71 | 28 | 100 |

SOURCE: Adapted from Shirley W. Y. Kuo, et al., _The Taiwan Success Story (1952-1979)_ (Boulder: Westview Press, 1981) Table 5.1.

labor-intensive growth path had a significant impact on not only the reduction of unemployment, but also on the improvement of the functional and overall distribution of income in Taiwan.

# CHAPTER V

## GROWTH AND HOUSEHOLD DISTRIBUTION OF INCOME (HID)

This paper has examined in Chapter III the intersectoral economic growth in relation to changes in economic factors in each sector as the economic center of gravity shifted from the agricultural to the nonagricultural sector. As a result, Korea's economy underwent significant changes in its structure of distribution between and within the sectors.

Intersectorally, the nonagricultural income (in real terms) grew seven times from 1961 to 1979, increasing at an annual rate of 11.5%, while the agricultural income increased only two and a half times at an annual rate of 4.2% during the same period as shown in Table 26 and Table 45. The rapid growth in nonagricultural income, relative to agricultural income, naturally resulted in a decline in the share of agricultural income from 37.9% in 1961 to 24.3% in 1970, and further to 18.2% in 1979 as shown in Table 26, column 5 and Table 46.

Intrasectorally, agricultural income was not functionally disaggregated into wage and property incomes. In the farm-family type of agricultural activity, such a separation would have entailed a rather arbitrary imputation procedure. For nonagricultural income, the functional distribution of wage and property income can, however,

TABLE 45

DISTRIBUTION OF NATIONAL INCOME, 1961-1979
(Unit: In billion 1970 won)

| (1) Year | (2) National Income (y=wL+rk+a) | (3) Wage Income (wL) | (4) Property Income (rk) | (5) Non-agricultural Income (v=wL+rk) | (6) Agricultural Income (a) |
|---|---|---|---|---|---|
| 1961 | 1,055.42 | 461.12 | 193.78 | 654.90 | 400.52 |
| 1962 | 1,061.40 | 486.08 | 218.25 | 704.33 | 357.06 |
| 1963 | 1,174.29 | 480.84 | 225.14 | 705.98 | 469.32 |
| 1964 | 1,296.63 | 497.33 | 247.02 | 744.35 | 552.28 |
| 1965 | 1,354.28 | 578.78 | 303.29 | 882.70 | 471.58 |
| 1966 | 1,500.27 | 667.29 | 348.40 | 1,015.69 | 484.58 |
| 1967 | 1,599.27 | 762.69 | 395.18 | 1,157.87 | 441.40 |
| 1968 | 1,761.19 | 856.50 | 456.59 | 1,313.09 | 448.08 |
| 1969 | 2,025.73 | 1,013.23 | 485.37 | 1,498.60 | 527.13 |
| 1970 | 2,256.25 | 1,145.77 | 562.40 | 1,708.17 | 548.08 |
| 1971 | 2,496.62 | 1,289.83 | 591.48 | 1,881.31 | 615.41 |
| 1972 | 2,657.75 | 1,370.41 | 642.51 | 2,012.92 | 644.84 |
| 1973 | 3,127.51 | 1,599.16 | 828.83 | 2,427.99 | 699.51 |
| 1974 | 3,494.55 | 1,738.03 | 960.38 | 2,698.41 | 796.15 |
| 1975 | 3,663.39 | 1,822.26 | 978.72 | 2,800.98 | 862.41 |
| 1976 | 4,222.88 | 2,115.63 | 1,147.81 | 3,263.44 | 959.43 |
| 1977 | 4,564.44 | 2,386.10 | 1,217.03 | 3,603.13 | 961.30 |
| 1978 | 5,135.42 | 2,768.93 | 1,337.54 | 4,106.47 | 1,028.95 |
| 1979 | 5,688.63 | 2,979.13 | 1,675.76 | 4,654.89 | 1,033.74 |
| Annual Growth Rate | 9.8 | 10.9 | 12.7 | 11.5 | 4.2 |

SOURCE: The Bank of Korea, Economic Statistics Yearbook (Seoul, 1977) and The Bank of Korea, Monthly Economic Statistics (Seoul, Jan. 1965-Jan. 1981).

NOTE: All incomes (factor cost) are deflated by GNP deflator based on 1970 won.

Nonagricultural income is functionally classified as wage and property income, but agricultural income is not. Rather, it is separated into an arbitrary imputation procesure.

The unincorporated income is divided into labor and capital components for each period in accordance with the current relationship between wage and property income in the entire economy excluding the unincorporated sector.

TABLE 46

DISTRIBUTIVE SHARES OF NATIONAL INCOME, 1961-1979
(Percent)

| (1) Year | (2) Wage Share ($s_W$) | (3) Property Share ($s_R$) | (4) Nonagricultural Share ($s_V$) | (5) Agricultural Share ($s_A$) | (6) Relative Share ($s_W/s_R$) | (7) Relative Share ($s_A/s_V$) |
|---|---|---|---|---|---|---|
| 1961 | .437 | .184 | .621 | .379 | 2.375 | .610 |
| 1962 | .458 | .206 | .664 | .336 | 2.223 | .506 |
| 1963 | .409 | .192 | .601 | .339 | 2.130 | .564 |
| 1964 | .383 | .191 | .574 | .426 | 2.005 | .742 |
| 1965 | .427 | .224 | .652 | .348 | 1.906 | .534 |
| 1966 | .445 | .232 | .667 | .323 | 1.918 | .484 |
| 1967 | .477 | .247 | .724 | .276 | 1.931 | .381 |
| 1968 | .486 | .259 | .746 | .254 | 1.876 | .340 |
| 1969 | .500 | .240 | .740 | .260 | 2.083 | .351 |
| 1970 | .508 | .249 | .757 | .243 | 2.040 | .321 |
| 1971 | .517 | .237 | .754 | .246 | 2.181 | .326 |
| 1972 | .516 | .242 | .757 | .243 | 2.132 | .321 |
| 1973 | .511 | .265 | .776 | .224 | 1.928 | .289 |
| 1974 | .497 | .275 | .772 | .228 | 1.807 | .295 |
| 1975 | .497 | .267 | .765 | .235 | 1.861 | .307 |
| 1976 | .501 | .272 | .773 | .227 | 1.842 | .294 |
| 1977 | .522 | .267 | .789 | .211 | 1.955 | .267 |
| 1978 | .539 | .261 | .800 | .200 | 2.065 | .250 |
| 1979 | .524 | .294 | .818 | .182 | 1.782 | .222 |

SOURCE: Table 45.

be explicitly separated and examined as was done in Chapter IV. Thus, the analysis of the functional distribution in Chapter IV indicates that the labor share of Korea's nonagricultural income has generally declined from 1961 through 1979. Wage and property incomes remarkably increased at an annual rate of 10.9% and 12.7%, respectively, during the period of 1961-1979 as shown in Table 45. The rapid increase in property income relative to wage income, however, led to a considerable decline of the labor share from 70.4% in 1961 to 67.1% in 1970 and further to 64.0% in 1979 as shown in Table 47. Such a worsening of the labor share in nonagricultural income resulted from the pattern of immoderate capital-intensive industrial growth and a tendency for labor-saving technological progress in the nonagricultural sector.

The purpose of this chapter is to link growth with inequality of income distribution, thus linking the sectoral and functional distributions with family distribution of income as a whole. In other words, this chapter attempts to trace the impact of changes in the structures of intersectoral and intrasectoral growths on the inequality of household distribution of income (HID) as a whole.

In analyzing the overall relationships between sectoral growths and HID (household distribution of income) in a dualistic developing economy, our factor decomposition model can be applied as a theoretical framework which has recently been developed by Fei, Ranis, and Kuo.[59]

---

[59]John C. H. Fei, Gustav Ranis, and Shirley W. Y. Kuo, Growth and Equity: The Taiwan Case (New York: Oxford University Press, 1979).

TABLE 47

FUNCTIONAL DISTRIBUTIVE SHARE OF NONAGRICULTURAL INCOME, 1961-1979
(Percent)

| (1) Year | (2) Wage Share ($s'_W$) | (3) Property Share ($s'_R$) | (4) Relative Share ($s'_W/s'_R$) | (5) Total ($s'_W+s'_R$) |
|---|---|---|---|---|
| 1961 | .704 | .296 | 2.378 | 1.000 |
| 1962 | .690 | .310 | 2.226 | 1.000 |
| 1963 | .681 | .319 | 2.136 | 1.000 |
| 1964 | .668 | .332 | 2.012 | 1.000 |
| 1965 | .656 | .344 | 1.907 | 1.000 |
| 1966 | .657 | .343 | 1.915 | 1.000 |
| 1967 | .659 | .341 | 1.933 | 1.000 |
| 1968 | .652 | .348 | 1.874 | 1.000 |
| 1969 | .676 | .324 | 2.086 | 1.000 |
| 1970 | .671 | .329 | 2.040 | 1.000 |
| 1971 | .686 | .314 | 2.185 | 1.000 |
| 1972 | .681 | .319 | 2.135 | 1.000 |
| 1973 | .659 | .341 | 1.933 | 1.000 |
| 1974 | .644 | .356 | 1.809 | 1.000 |
| 1975 | .651 | .349 | 1.865 | 1.000 |
| 1976 | .648 | .352 | 1.841 | 1.000 |
| 1977 | .662 | .338 | 1.959 | 1.000 |
| 1978 | .674 | .326 | 2.067 | 1.000 |
| 1979 | .640 | .360 | 1.778 | 1.000 |

SOURCE: Table 45.

NOTE: $s'_W = s_W/s_V$ and $s'_R = s_R/s_V$.

In their analytical framework, the gradual reallocation of labor between the sectors (sectoral distribution of income) and the changes in technological progress and capital accumulation within the sector (functional distribution of income) can be regarded as major factor components of changes in inequality of HID. Thus, the changes in inequality measure, Gini coefficient, over time can be traced as a growth-relevant issue in this paper. In particular, our factor decomposition framework enables allocating the multiple causes of any change in inequality of HID through time to a reallocation effect, a functional distribution effect, and a factor Gini effect. Empirical results of this chapter center on estimation of the importance of those effects in the case of Korea's experience during the past twenty years.

The first section of this paper will briefly mention methodology for the analysis of additive factor components. The actual historical experience of inequality is introduced in the second section and the quantitative effects of growth on HID will be traced and analyzed in the third section.

## Methodology of Additive Factor Components

One of the well-known inequality measures may be expressed as the Gini coefficient. This Gini coefficient will be used here as the indicator of income inequality; the greater the Gini coefficient, the less even the income distribution. Admissible values of the Gini coefficient range from 0 to 1.

As shown in Figure 11, the Gini coefficient of income Y is defined as the ratio of the area enclosed by the diagonal line and the Lorenz curve to the area of the triangle, namely the shaded area OAC to the area of triangle OAB. The Gini coefficient of each factor income component can be calculated simply by the following equation:[60]

$$J_Y = \frac{2}{n} (1\ y_1 + 2\ y_2 + \ldots + n\ y_n) - \frac{n+1}{n} \qquad (26)$$

where $J_y$: Gini coefficient of subscript income Y

and $y_i$: the percentage share of the ith family income,

thus, $y_1 + y_2 + \ldots + y_n = 1$ and

$y_1 \leq y_2 \leq \ldots \leq y_n$.

(The percentage share of family incomes is arranged in a monotonically nondecreasing order, so that the first family is the poorest and the last family, the richest.)

According to Equation 26, one may estimate Gini coefficients of any type of factor income components in the system of the economy: national income Gini, wage income Gini, property income Gini, agricultural income Gini, and even transfer income Gini.

For the sake of convenience, income can be decomposed into the above factor components according to a classification of the sources of income: that is, according to components of the sectoral distribution of income and the functional distribution of income. Thus, national income can be disaggregated into nonagricultural and

---

[60]Ibid., p. 330.

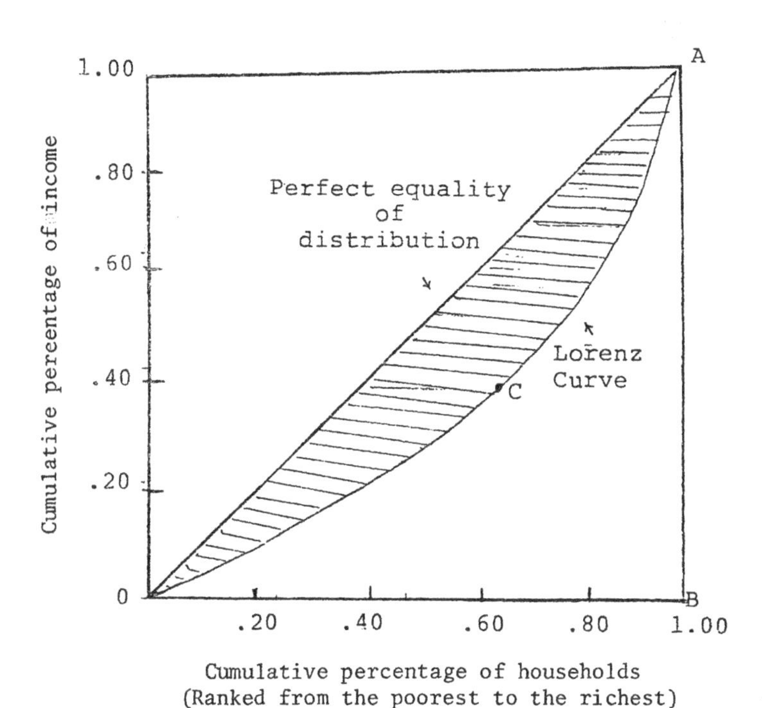


Fig. 11. Gini coefficient and Lorenz curve. Diagrammatically, a Lorenz curve is derived by plotting the cumulative percentage share of income received, shown on the vertical axis, against the cumulative percentage of the households, shown on the horizontal axis. The diagonal line represents the perfect equality of income distribution when Gini coefficient equals zero. Gini coefficient = area AOC/area AOB.

agricultural income, and the nonagricultural income, into wage and property income as follows:

$$Y = V + A \tag{27}$$

$$V = W + R \tag{28}$$

and $$Y = W + R + A \tag{29}$$

where Y: national income

V: nonagricultural income

A: agricultural income

W: wage income

and R: property income.

A factor decomposition model can then be introduced by the linkage of the inequality of total income with the inequality of factor income components and their corresponding shares in total income. That is, total income inequality is defined as the sum of the weighted factor Ginis where the weights are the distributive shares of factor income in total income. This is systematically and rigorously developed in Growth with Equity written by Fei, Ranis, and Kuo.[61] Here, we shall restrict ourselves to summarizing the results in the form of the following equation:

$$J_Y = s_V J_V + s_A J_A - s_T J_T - e \tag{30}$$

---

[61]Ibid.

where s and J stand for the factor share in total national income and the Gini coefficient of each subscript, respectively. T is the transfer income (welfare income) and e, an error term.

The Gini coefficient of total national income can be determined by the forces of the weighted average of the three factor Ginis and an error: nonagricultural income Gini ($J_V$), agricultural income Gini ($J_A$), transfer income Gini ($J_T$), and one error term (e).

For the sake of convenience, one may classify income into three types of factor income components; Type 1 income, Type 2 income, and Type 3 income.[62] The specific characteristics of Type 1 income are that a richer family has both absolutely and proportionately more of such income than a poorer family; property income is usually a good example. A characteristic of Type 2 income is that a richer family has absolutely more, but proportionately less of such income than the poorer family; wage income is a good example. Consequently, Type 1 income is distributed less equally than total national income, and Type 2 income, more equally than total national income.

With respect to Type 3 income, it should be noted that a negative sign is attached to it in Equation 30. This is because the

---

[62] Income can be classified into three types of income in terms of the signs of the intercept $a_i$ and the slope $b_i$ in the linear regression between the decile families of each factor income component and of total income:

$$V = \hat{a}_V + \hat{b}_V Y: \quad \begin{array}{l} \hat{a}_V < 0,\ \hat{b}_V > 0, \text{ Type 1 income} \\ \hat{a}_V > 0,\ \hat{b}_V > 0, \text{ Type 2 income} \\ \hat{a}_V > 0,\ \hat{b}_V < 0, \text{ Type 3 income.} \end{array}$$

Fei, et al., Growth with Equity, pp. 363-364.

distinguishing characteristic of Type 3 income is that it decreases absolutely for richer families. That is, it is an income distribution equalizer; transfer income (welfare income) is a typical example.

In Korea's experience, however, Type 3 income (welfare income) is small and negligible because Korea did not have any distinguishable welfare program. In addition, the error term "e" in Equation 30 tends to be small or negligible when the linear correlation between each factor income component and total income are nearly perfect or close to one.

Hence, assuming that the above two terms in the equation are small or negligible, our factor decomposition model (Equation 30) can be confined to the use of an approximation equation in which the overall Gini coefficient is simplified to the weighted sum of Type 1 and Type 2 incomes:

$$J_Y = s_V J_V + s_A J_A \qquad (31)$$
$$(s_V + s_A = 1).$$

In the same fashion, Equations 28 and 29 can be expressed, respectively, as follows:

$$J_V = s'_W J_W + s'_R J_R \qquad (32)$$
$$(s'_W + s'_R + 1)$$

and $$J_Y = s_W J_W + s_R J_R + s_A J_A \qquad (33)$$
$$(s_W + s_R + s_A = 1)$$

where $s_W = s_V s'_W$ and $s_R = s_V s'_R$ .

Now, one may differentiate the above three equations (31, 32, and 33) with respect to time t and arrange the results. A following differential equation can then be rewritten:

$$\frac{dJ_Y}{dt} = (J_A - J_V)\ ds_A/dt + (J_W - J_R)\ s_V\ ds'_W/dt + s_A\ dJ_A/dt + s_W\ dJ_W/dt + s_R\ dJ_R/dt \quad (34)$$

$$\left(\text{or } \frac{dJ_Y}{dt} = R + D + B\right)$$

where the causation of changes in $J_Y$ (overall distribution of income) over time can be attributed to three forces: such as 1) intersectoral reallocation effect (R); 2) functional distrubtion effect (D); and 3) factor Gini effect (B):

1) $R = (J_A - J_V)\ ds_A/dt$

2) $D = (J_W - J_R)\ s_V\ ds'_W/dt$, and

3) $B = s_A\ dJ_A/dt + s_W\ dJ_W/dt + s_R\ dJ_R/dt$.

The first two effects are growth-relevant effects. Intersectoral reallocation effect (R) reflects the importance of a continuous shift of the economy's center of gravity from its agricultural to its nonagricultural sector. This shift can be proxied by a decline in $S_A$, the share of agricultural income in total national income in the course of industrialization.

In the course of intersectoral resource reallocation in the dualistic developing economy, the distributive share of agricultural income in total national income usually declines through time, that is,

$ds_A/dt$ is less than zero. Thus, the impact of the intersectoral reallocation effect on the overall distribution of income ($J_Y$) depends upon the sign of $J_A$-$J_V$. If $J_A$-$J_V < 0$, for instance, agricultural income is distributed more equally than nonagricultural income, then the intersectoral reallocation effect (R) will increase the overall inequality of the distribution of income (positive effect on the overall Gini $J_Y$).

Conversely, the intersectoral reallocation effect reduces the overall inequality of HID, or household distribution of income, when agricultural income is less equally distributed than nonagricultural income ($J_A - J_V > 0$) and the distributive share of agricultural income in total national income declines over time, such as $ds_A/dt < 0$.

In the same fashion, the functional distribution effect (D) describes changes in $J_Y$ due to changes in the relative shares of capital and labor. Wage income is usually distributed more equally than property income (wage income is a Type 2 income), so that $J_W - J_R < 0$. Then, a change in the functional distribution in favor of labor or increasing $s'_W$, will always serve to improve the overall distribution of income.

Growth in the relative shares of labor in nonagricultural income can, in turn, be tied up with the existing theory of development. In the case of the labor surplus economy, as in Korea, wage may be assumed to be rising after the economic turning point due to a shortage in the labor force and a drastic increase in capital stock in the industrial sector. In this relation, the growth equation relevant to the direction of change in $s'_W$ after the turning point is given as follows:

$$G_{s'_W} = (1-s'_W)\ G_{K/L}\ (\frac{1}{\sigma} - 1) + B_L \qquad (35)^{63}$$

where $G_{K/L}$ : the growth rate of capital labor ratio,

$\sigma$ : the elasticity of substitution, and

$B_L$ : the degree of labor using biased technological progress in Hicks-nonneutral terms.

When we substitute Equation 35 in the functional distribution effect (D), the functional distribution effect can be rewritten as follows:

$$D = (J_W-J_R)\ s'_W s_V\ [(1-s'_W)\ G_{K/L}\ (\frac{1}{\sigma} - 1) + B_L] \qquad (36)$$

where the above functional distribution effect (D) can be explained in terms of changes in capital intensity ($G_{K/L}$), nonnuetral technological parameter ($\sigma$), and labor-using biased technological progress ($B_L$) along with the labor share and the difference between wage Gini ($J_W$) and property Gini ($J_R$).

In this relation, the functional distribution effect (D) reduces the overall income inequality of HID when the underlying conditions of growth improve the labor share; $ds'_W/dt > 0$ if and only if $J_W-J_R < 0$.

As far as the factor Gini effect (B) is concerned, any improvement in the equality of any factor income component will

---

[63]Fei, et al., Growth with Equity, p. 85 and Fei and Ranis, Labor Surplus Economy.

serve to improve the overall household distribution of income as a whole. The factor Gini effect B, which is composed of the weighted changes in three factor income Ginis, will contribute to greater HID equality if the net effect is a negative sign on B. A negative B may be caused by a change in the asset ownership patterns of either capital or labor or both. A more equal capital ownership pattern can result from the fact that lower income households acquire capital assets faster than the wealthier families, or the fact that there is a land or capital reform.

The pattern of ownership of labor income, on the other hand, can become more equal over time, when lower income families manage to acquire more skilled labor through their own educational expenditures or the government's provision of education to the lower income groups.

In this way, the factor decomposition equation provides us with a framework for the analysis of the impact of growth on HID within a dualistic developing economy. In the next two sections, the actual historical experience of inequalities will be examined, and this framework will be applied to Korea's economy.

## Korea's Experience of Inequalities

In the examination of inequalities, the overall households are classified into agricultural and nonagricultural. The nonagricultural households are further classified into employer and employee households, especially for the decomposition analysis.

The two common inequality measures for each classified sector are investigated: the decile distribution ratio and the Gini coefficient. The inequality data collected by KDI (Korea Development Institute) will be used for the years of 1965, 1970, and 1976 as the bench mark years.

Inequality data for the early 1960s are not available, so that we cannot see the trend in that period. We note, however, that during the period 1965-1970 a slight tendency toward improvement in overall HID occurred but that a rapid deterioration followed in the years 1970-1976.

As shown in Table 48, this trend is evident in the two distributive measures. The decile distribution ratio (A/C) in Table 48, column 5, slightly increases from .450 in 1965 to .472 in 1970 and then decreases drastically to .372 in 1976. During the years 1965 and 1970, the relative shares of the bottom 40% and the middle 40% slightly increased by 1.9% and 2.2%, respectively, while that of the top 20% decreased by 2.8% from 1965 to 1970. Thus, a certain amount of the income of the top 20% smoothly moved to both the bottom and the middle income groups, but more to the middle 40% than to the bottom 40% group.

From 1970 to 1976, however, the situation has been completely reversed. The income shares of both the bottom 40% and the middle 40% drastically decreased by 14.2% and 2.4%, respectively, while that of the top 20% largely increased by 8.9%. It should be noted that a great portion of the increases in the income share of the top 20% resulted from a large percent decrease in that of the bottom 40%. Consequently, the overall distribution of income which deteriorated

TABLE 48

OVERALL HOUSEHOLD DISTRIBUTION OF INCOME IN KOREA, 1965-1976

| (1) Year | (2) Bottom 40% (A) % | (3) Middle 40% (B) % | (4) Top 20% (C) % | (5) Decile Ratio (A/C) | (6) Overall Gini ($J_y$) |
|---|---|---|---|---|---|
| 1965 | 19.25 | 37.93 | 42.82 | .450 | .343 |
| 1970 | 19.63 | 38.75 | 41.62 | .472 | .332 |
| 1976 | 16.85 | 37.81 | 45.34 | .372 | .381 |

SOURCE: Adapted from Hakchung Choo and Daemo Kim, Probable Size Distribution of Income in Korea (Seoul: KDI, 1978) and Toshiuki Mizoguchi, Do Hyung Kim, and Young Il Chung, "Overtime Changes of the Size Distribution of Household Income in Korea, 1963-1971," The Developing Economics, Vol. XIV, No. 3 (Sept. 1976).

from 1970 to 1976 reached a level even worse than that of 1965.

The overall Gini coefficient ($J_Y$) improved from .343 in 1965 to .332 in 1970, and then deteriorated abruptly to .381 in 1976. It is evident from all the above measures of inequality that the distribution income improved slightly during the period 1965-1970 and then deteriorated sharply during the period of 1970-1976. In addition, it is clearly seen that the deterioration of both the overall Gini coefficient and the decile ratio in 1976 is much worse than that of 1965.

Agricultural distribution of income, shown in Table 49, indicates a trend toward widening the gaps within this sector. The decile distribution ratio (A/C) continually decreases from .595 in 1965 to .550 in 1970, and further to .479 in 1976. The income share of the middle 40% slightly fluctuated around 40%, but the share of the bottom 40% decreased from 22.63% in 1965 to 21.24% in 1970 and further to 19.45% in 1976. On the other hand, the share of the top 20% steadily increased from 38.03% in 1965 to 38.64% in 1970, and further to 40.62% in 1976. Consequently, the distribution of agricultural household income has shown an increasing trend in inequality of the Gini coefficient from .285 in 1965 to .294 in 1970, and further to .327 in 1976.

Between the sectors, however, the agricultural income has been distributed more evenly than either nonagricultural income or overall household income. That is, agricultural income was of Type 2. Therefore, the Gini coefficients for agricultural households were lower than those for both nonagricultural households and overall

TABLE 49

AGRICULTURAL HOUSEHOLD DISTRIBUTION OF INCOME IN KOREA, 1965-1976

| (1) Year | (2) Bottom 40% (A) % | (3) Middle 40% (B) % | (4) Top 20% (C) % | (5) Decile Ratio (A/C) | (6) Gini ($J_A$) |
|---|---|---|---|---|---|
| 1965 | 22.63 | 39.34 | 38.03 | .595 | .285 |
| 1970 | 21.24 | 40.12 | 38.64 | .550 | .294 |
| 1976 | 19.45 | 39.93 | 40.62 | .479 | .327 |

SOURCE: Same as Table 48.

HID in all three periods.

As a result, the worsening of rural income distribution and the decline of the relative importance of the agricultural sector (the decrease in agricultural income share) would have an unfavorable effect on the improvement in the overall distribution of income.

The trend in the distribution of income for nonagricultural households for the years of 1965, 1970, and 1976 corresponds with the general trend observed in the overall distribution of income. Within this sector, the income share of the bottom 40% increased by 12.3% from the 16.95% share in 1965 to a 18.87% share in 1970. At the same time, the share of the middle 40% also increased by 5.3% from the 36.18% share in 1965 to a 38.09% in 1970 as shown in Table 50. On the other hand, the share of the top 20% decreased by 8.2% from 46.87% in 1965 to 43.04% in 1970. Consequently, the decile ratio increased from .362 in 1965 to .438 in 1970 and the Gini coefficient for these households improved by a decreasing trend in inequality from .388 in 1965 to .346 in 1970. According to these trends in the two inequality measures, the distribution of nonagricultural income improved during the period 1965-1970.

However, the distribution of nonagricultural income deteriorated sharply from 1970 to 1976. The decile ratio dropped from .438 in 1970 to .315 in 1976 which implies that the share of the bottom 40% decreased relative to that of the top 20%. The share of the bottom 40% decreased sharply by 18.6% from the 18.87% share in 1970 to the 15.36% share in 1976. The share of the middle 40%

TABLE 50

NONAGRICULTURAL HOUSEHOLD DISTRIBUTION OF INCOME IN KOREA, 1965-1976

| (1)<br>Year | (2)<br>Bottom<br>40%<br>(A)<br>% | (3)<br>Middle<br>40%<br>(B)<br>% | (4)<br>Top<br>20%<br>(C)<br>% | (5)<br>Decile<br>Ratio<br>(A/C) | (6)<br>Gini<br>($J_V$) |
|---|---|---|---|---|---|
| 1965 | 16.95 | 36.18 | 46.87 | .362 | .388 |
| 1970 | 18.87 | 38.09 | 43.04 | .438 | .346 |
| 1976 | 15.36 | 35.94 | 48.70 | .315 | .412 |

SOURCE: Same as Table 48.

also decreased by 5.6% from 38.09% in 1970 to 35.94% in 1976. Thus, the share of the bottom 40% was much worse than that of the middle 40% in 1976.

On the other hand, the share of the top 20% increased drastically by 13.1% from 43.04% in 1970 to 48.70% in 1976. Therefore, the nonagricultural income was much more concentrated on the top 20% in 1976 than in 1970. This level was even much worse than that of 1965. As a result, the Gini coefficient increased from .346 in 1970 to .412 in 1976 which indicates that the distribution of nonagricultural income deteriorated in the period of 1970-1976.

Between the agricultural and nonagricultural sectors, the shares of the bottom 40% and the middle 40% in the nonagricultural sector were lower than those of the same income groups in the agricultural sector in each corresponding year. On the other hand, the share of the top 20% in the nonagricultural sector was much higher than that of the same income group in the agricultural sector in each year. This indicates that the nonagricultural income was much more centralized on the top 20% than the agricultural income.

Consequently, the income of nonagricultural households was distributed less equally than that of the agricultural sector and of even all households. That is, Korea's nonagricultural income was of Type 1. The Gini coefficient for the distribution of nonagricultural income in each corresponding period was much higher than that for agricultural income distribution and for overall HID. In this relation, the overall distribution of income would have deteriorated by the increase in the share of nonagricultural income in national income as the economic center of gravity shifted from agricultural to nonagricultural activities.

For the convenience of the decomposition analysis, an attempt was made to classify nonagricultural households into wage households and property households. The results of this attempt are also shown in Tables 51 and 52.

The distribution of wage income improved very much from 1965 to 1970, and then deteriorated from 1970 to 1976. The deterioration, however, was not as bad as that of 1965. From 1965 to 1970, most significant is the increase in the share of the bottom 40% due to the decline in both the shares of the middle 40% and of the top 20%. Thus, the decile ratio improved from .331 in 1965 to .531 in 1970 and the Gini coefficients for wage households improved by the decline of inequality from .399 to .304 in the same period.

From 1970 to 1976, however, the decile ratio and the Gini coefficient deteriorated from .531 and .304 in 1970 to .427 and .355 in 1976, respectively, due to the decline in the shares of the bottom 40% and of the middle 40%.

The distribution of property income had much the same trend in each income group as that of wage income. However, the difference was that the deterioration of property income distribution after 1970 was much worse than that of before 1970. And another important factor between the two sectors is that the property income was distributed more equally than the wage income in 1965. Therefore, the property Gini coefficient (.384) was lower than the wage Gini coeffi-

TABLE 51

DISTRIBUTION OF WAGE INCOME, 1965-1976

| (1) Year | (2) Bottom 40% (A) % | (3) Middle 40% (B) % | (4) Top 20% (C) % | (5) Decile Ratio (A/C) | (6) Gini ($J_W$) |
|---|---|---|---|---|---|
| 1965 | 14.49 | 41.71 | 43.80 | .331 | .399 |
| 1970 | 20.76 | 40.14 | 39.10 | .531 | .304 |
| 1976 | 18.52 | 38.13 | 43.35 | .427 | .355 |

SOURCE: Same as Table 48.

TABLE 52

DISTRIBUTION OF PROPERTY INCOME, 1965-1976

| (1) Year | (2) Bottom 40% (A) % | (3) Middle 40% (B) % | (4) Top 20% (C) % | (5) Decile Ratio (A/C) | (6) Gini ($J_R$) |
|---|---|---|---|---|---|
| 1965 | 15.22 | 41.69 | 43.09 | .353 | .384 |
| 1970 | 17.62 | 40.36 | 42.02 | .419 | .353 |
| 1976 | 11.35 | 40.28 | 48.31 | .235 | .449 |

SOURCE: Same as Table 48.

cient (.399) so that the property income was of Type 2 in 1965.

However, both in 1970 and in 1976, the property income was distributed less evenly than the wage income so that the property income changed to Type 1 income. Thus, the Gini coefficients of property households were higher than those of wage households in both periods.

In sum, the changes in income type, each sector's inequality, and the relative importance of economic activities between the sectors would have a great impact on the overall distribution of income. As a result, Korea experienced a particular distribution of income, a U-shaped pattern in the course of economic growth, rather than the inverse U-shaped pattern which was hypothesized by Kuznets and Myrdal.[64]

The next section will focus on an examination of the effects of economic growth on the overall distribution of income by tracing the causation of the actual inequality pattern back to Korea's particular growth path.

---

[64]Kuznets (1955, 1963) and Myrdal (1957) hypothesized that the processes of industrialization and urbanization lead to a worsening of income distribution in developing countries. The reason is because in the early stages, growth is concentrated in the modern sectors. Thereafter the distribution improves in the course of economic growth. Thus, there is an adverse relationship between distribution (Gini inequality measure or the share of the top 20% income) and growth (GNP per capita) in the early stages of development, and thereafter a favorable relationship between them (the inverse U-shaped pattern). Chenery tested the inverse U-shaped hypothesis by fitting the quadratic equation to cross-country data. In this model, the share of the top 20% income (as a dependent variable) was explained by the GNP per capita (an independent variable).

Hollis B. Chenery, ed., Redistribution with Growth (London: Oxford University Press, 1974).

## The Effects of Growth on the Overall HID

### Empirical Application to Korea

Korea has achieved an unprecedented record of economic growth since the early 1960s while simultaneously experiencing an improvement in the overall distribution of income until 1970. But thereafter the distribution of income deteriorated during the period of continued rapid growth. Thus, Korea's overall distribution of income experienced a U-shaped pattern in the course of economic growth during the past two decades.

In order to find out the cause of the U-shaped pattern of distribution, this paper will link the economic growth to the distribution of income by attributing the actual inequality of overall HID to Korea's particular growth pattern. Thus, the path of inequality measure (Gini coefficient) affected by the particular forces of growth can be decomposed into three main types of effects: intersectoral reallocation effect, functional distribution effect, and factor Gini effect. We have identified those effects in the first section of this chapter.

For the convenience of analysis, the period of 1965-1976 is divided into two phases; before and after 1970. Table 53 summarizes the factor Gini coefficients for each of the factor income components ($J_W$, $J_R$, and $J_A$) along with the overall Gini coefficient ($J_Y$). The distributive shares for each of the factor components are also found in the same table.

TABLE 53

GINI COEFFICIENTS OF FACTOR INCOME COMPONENTS AND THEIR SHARES, 1965-1976

| Variables | 1965 | 1970 | 1976 |
|---|---|---|---|
| Overall Gini ($J_Y$). . . . . . . . | .343 | .332 | .381 |
| Wage Gini ($J_W$) . . . . . . . . . | .399 | .304 | .355 |
| Property Gini ($J_R$) . . . . . . . | .384 | .353 | .449 |
| Agricultural Gini ($J_A$) . . . . . | .285 | .294 | .327 |
| Nonagricultural Gini ($J_V$). . . . | .388 | .346 | .412 |
| Wage Share ($s_W$). . . . . . . . . | .427 | .508 | .501 |
| Property Share ($s_R$). . . . . . . | .225 | .249 | .272 |
| Agricultural Share ($s_A$). . . . . | .348 | .243 | .227 |
| Nonagricultural Share ($s_V$) . . . | .652 | .757 | .773 |

SOURCE: Data for Ginis from Tables 48-52. Data for shares from Tables 46-47.

NOTE: $s'_W = s_W/s_V$ and $s'_R = s_R/s_V$.

Intersectoral Reallocation Effect (R)

The essence of development in the dualistic economy as in Korea is the gradual reallocation of resources, particularly labor from agricultural to nonagricultural activities. The third section of Chapter II involves Korea's gradual labor transfer in terms of the labor absorption in the nonagricultural sector in the coures of urban industrialization.

When Korea's economy developed and the rural labor force was reallocated, the modern sector expanded rapidly while the rural sector shrunk significantly. Therefore, since the early 1960s, agricultural income grew at a slower rate than nonagricultural income in the development process.

This rapid industrialization resulted in widening of the income gap between the two sectors for the past two decades. Table 53 shows that the distributive share of agricultural income ($s_A$) consistently declined from 34.8% in 1965 to 24.3% in 1970, and further to 22.7% in 1976 as the economic center of gravity shifted from agricultural to nonagricultural sector. In mathematical terms, this is simply expressed as $ds_A/dt < 0$.

In addition, in terms of the degree of income inequality within each sector, the income was more equally distributed in the agricultural sector than in nonagricultural sector for the entire period. In other words, agricultural income was Type 2 income, while nonagricultural income was Type 1 income both before and after 1970. Therefore, this is simply expressed as $J_A - J_V < 0$.

In the decomposition model of Equation 34, the reallocation

effect (R) is defined as the product of $J_A - J_V < 0$ and $ds_A/dt < 0$. Therefore, the reallocation effect (R) had a positive impact on the Gini coefficient of overall HID which implies an increase in inequality of overall Gini $J_Y$.

R (reallocation effect) in Table 54 is calculated as +.0108 before 1970 and +.0008 after 1970. Thus, the positive reallocation effect contributed to the great inequality of overall HID before and after 1970, but the effect before 1970 was much stronger than that after 1970.

Functional Distribution Effect (D)

The functional distribution between capital and labor in the nonagricultural sector has been heavily discussed in relation to the aggregate CES production function in the previous chapter. Chapter IV attempted to quantify the neutral and nonneutral parameters of the production function which are related to the relative factor shares between capital and labor.

The analysis of the production explored trends in capital intensity, the direction of capital-biased technological progress, and an increase in the elasticity of substitution of capital for labor, all of which contributed to the determination of an increase in capital share in the nonagricultural sector.

In Equation 36, the functional distribution effect D can be separated into two parts, the Gini inequality term and the growth-relevant term. The former is defined as the difference between $J_W$ and $J_R$. The latter is determined by capital-intensity ($G_{K/L}$), elasticity of substitution of capital for labor ($\sigma$), and the direction

TABLE 54

EFFECTS OF REALLOCATION, FUNCTIONAL DISTRIBUTION, AND FACTOR GINI ON OVERALL DISTRIBUTION OF INCOME, 1965-1976

| Variable | Notation | Total Estimated Change | | Percentage Distribution of Estminated Change | |
|---|---|---|---|---|---|
| | | 1965-1970 | 1970-1976 | 1965-1970 (%) | 1970-1976 (%) |
| Overall Gini | $dJ_Y$ | -.0335 | +.0595 | 100.0 | 100.0 |
| Reallocation Effect | R | .0108 | .0008 | 32.2 | 1.3 |
| Functional Distribution Effect | D | .0002 | .0009 | .6 | 1.5 |
| Factor Gini Effect | B | -.0445 | .0578 | -132.8 | 97.2 |
| Agricultural Gini | $J_AE$ | .0031 | .0080 | 9.3 | 13.5 |
| Nonagricultural Gini | $J_VE$ | -.0476 | .0498 | -142.1 | 83.7 |
| Wage Gini | $J_WE$ | -.0406 | .0259 | -121.2 | 43.5 |
| Property Gini | $J_RE$ | -.0070 | .0239 | - 20.9 | 40.2 |

SOURCE: Calculated according to the differential decomposition equation (Equation 34, $dJ_Y = R + D + B$) on the base of data in Table 53.

NOTE: $dJ_Y = R + D + B$ and $B = J_AE + J_VE$, where $J_VE = J_WE + J_RE$. JE stands for effect of J's subscript.

of factor-biased technological progress ($B_L$) along with the labor share ($s'_W$).

Based on the mathematical expression of the functional distribution effect, $D = (J_W - J_R)\ s_V\ ds'_W/dt$, the growth-relevant term, $s'_W s_V\ [(1 - s'_W)G_{K/L}\ (\frac{1}{\sigma} - 1) + B_L]$ in Equation 36, is a proxy variable for $s_V ds'_W/dt$, namely, the change in the wage share in nonagricultural income over time. Thus, the growth-relevant term in Equation 36 could determine the change in the wage income share in terms of economic growth through time. In other words, the change in the relative share of wage income resulted from the change in the structure of economic growth in the nonagricultural sector.

In this relation, Korea's nonagricultural economy experienced trends in strong capital intensity and sustained labor-saving technological progress during the period of 1961-1976 except for the subperiod of 1965-1970. Accordingly, the relative share of wage income ($s'_W s_V = s_W$) increased from 42.7% in 1965 to 50.8% in 1970, and then decreased again to 50.1% in 1976 as shown in Table 53 and 55. In mathematical terms, these are simply expressed as $s_V ds'_W > 0$ for the period 1965-1970 and $s_V ds'_W < 0$ for the period 1970-1976.

There is the other factor to determine the functional distribution effect in terms of the degree of income inequality within each factor income component. The wage Gini coefficient (.399) was considerably larger than the property Gini coefficient (.384) before 1970 and thereafter turned out to be smaller than the property Gini coefficient as shown in Table 53. In other words, wage income was of Type 1 before 1970 and switched to Type 2 income after 1970. The

TABLE 55

EFFECT OF FUNCTIONAL DISTRIBUTION ON OVERALL DISTRIBUTION OF INCOME, 1965-1979

| Variable Notation | 1965-1970 | 1970-1976 | 1976-1979 |
|---|---|---|---|
| D | +.0002 | +.0009 | +.0005 |
| $(J_W - J_R)$ | .0150 | -.0490 | -.0940 |
| $(s'_W s_V)$ | .427 | .508 | .501 |
| $(1 - s'_W)$ | .344 | .329 | .352 |
| $(G_{K/L})$ | .0808 | .0403 | .0704 |
| $(\frac{1}{\sigma} - 1)$ | .3210 | .1136 | .1136 |
| $(B_L)$ | +.0158 | -.0357 | -.0134 |

NOTE: D (functional distribution effect) is calculated according to Equation 36:

$$D = (J_W - J_R)\ s'_W s_V\ [(1 - s'_w)\ G_{k/L}\ (\frac{1}{\sigma} - 1) + B_L]$$

$B_L$ = +.0158: Labor-using technological progress. $B_L$ = -.0357: Labor-saving technological progress.

difference between the two Ginis for each period can be expressed as $J_W - J_R > 0$ for the period 1965-1970 and $J_W - J_R < 0$ for the period 1970-1976.

Finally, we can calculate the functional distribution effect D by the product of the change in wage share (growth-relevant term) and the difference between wage and property Ginis for each corresponding period:

| | $J_W - J_R$ | $s_V ds'_W/dt$ | effect |
|---|---|---|---|
| 1965-1970 | + | + | + |
| 1970-1976 | - | - | + |

For the period 1965-1970, the income for the wage households was distributed less equally than that for the property households. The wage income, however, increased relatively faster than the property income. It is reasonable that such a situation necessarily contributed to the positive effect on the inequality of overall distribution of income.

During the period 1970-1976, wage income was distributed more equally than property income, but the well-distributed wage income significantly decreased relative to the property income. This also resulted in positive effect on the inequality of overall distribution income.

In Table 55, the functional distribution effect D is measured in terms of economic growth. According to the calculation, D is determined as +.0002 for the period 1965-1970 and +.0009 for the period 1970-1976. Thus, the functional distribution effect both before and after 1970 had an unfavorable impact on the overall households distribution of income, but the effect before 1970 was not as significant as that after 1970.

Factor Gini Effect (B)

The factor Gini effect is defined as the summation of the product of each factor share of agricultural, wage, and property income and each change in its corresponding Gini coefficient. Each factor income component has a different impact on the overall Gini $J_Y$ due to the change in each factor Gini and its corresponding share. We will first concentrate on the agricultural Gini effect, and then on the nonagricultural Gini effect, that is, the sum of wage Gini and property Gini effects.

The distribution of agricultural income continually deteriorated by an increase in its Gini inequality so that the factor Gini effect caused by agricultural income was always unfavorable to the overall household distribution of income both before and after 1970. Thus, the agricultural Gini effect is shown as +.0031 before 1970 and +.0080 after 1970 in Table 54.

However, the unfavorable agricultural Gini effect was not the dominant causative factor of change in the overal Gini $J_Y$ both before and after 1970. The reason is that in the course of rapid economic growth, the share of agricultural income in national income decreased from 35% in 1965 to 24% in 1970, and further to 23% in 1976. In addition, agricultural income always maintained Type 2 income which was distributed more equally than any other factor income component. Accordingly, the impact of the agricultural income Gini on the overall Gini $J_Y$ was relatively small, that is, 9.3% and 13.5% before and after 1970, respectively.

However, the nonagricultural Gini effect, which is the sum of wage Gini and property Gini effects, became a major causative factor of change in the overall distribution of income both before and after 1970. Before 1970, the highly favorable nonagricultural Gini effect ($J_V$E: -.0476 or -142.1%) overwhelmed not only the unfavorable agricultural Gini effect ($J_A$E: +.0031 or 9.3%) but also any other type of effect, so that the net effect resulted in the favorable change in the overall Gini $J_Y$ (-.0335) for the period 1965-1970.

After 1970, this situation was completely reversed. The drastic increases in both inequality of nonagricultural income and its large share in the national income inevitably led to the most unfavorable effect ($J_V$E: +.0498 or 83.7%) on the overall distribution of income along with other unfavorable effects for the period of 1970-1976. Thus, all the unfavorable effects add up to +.0595 for the same period.

For the sake of convenience, an attempt was made to separate the nonagricultural Gini effect into wage Gini effect and property Gini effect as shown in Table 54.

The distribution of wage income improved surprisingly by a remarkable decline in its Gini inequality from .399 in 1965 to .304 in 1970 and by a considerable increase in its share in national income. This brought about an enormous negative effect (-.0406) on the overall Gini inequality $J_Y$.

As far as the improvement in the wage income equality is concerned, low income families might manage to acquire more skilled labor through on-the-job training and their own education which would result in the pattern of ownership of labor income becoming more equal through time. Thus, the most favorable wage Gini effect (-.0406 or -121.2%) resulting from the large negative change in wage Gini multiplied by the relatively large share of wage income overwhelmingly exceeded the other unfavorable effects to improve the overall HID for the period 1965-1970.

After 1970, the income distribution for wage households deteriorated by an increase in its inequality from .304 in 1970 to .355 in 1976. The reason was not clear but it might be that the degree of labor force heterogeneity, based on high educational improvement, skill, age, and sex, became greater in the course of drastic urban-industrialization. Thus, the largest positive effect of wage Gini (+.0259 or 43.5%) contributed to the highly unfavorable overall distribution of income for the period 1970-1976.

With respect to the property Gini effect, the distribution of property income also improved by a decline in its Gini inequality from .384 in 1965 to .353 in 1970. The product of the negative change in property Gini and the property share is calculated as -.007, which would still contribute to more quality of overall HID. It might be caused by the change in Korea's asset ownership pattern of capital.

According to the data on the ownership of Korea's listed capital stock from 1966 to 1970, the distribution of capital stock ownership between corporations (entrepreneurs) and individuals (nonentrepreneurs) improved significantly.[65] The percentage of the individual ownership of capital stock increased by 129% while that of corporations' decreased by 22.9% for the same period. In addition, this period was one of high interest rates; the low and middle income groups were encouraged to save right after the high interest rate reform of September 1965. These would affect the improvement in the distribution of property income and consequently contribute to the favorable overall distribution of income during the period 1965-1970.

After 1970, the distribution of property income deteriorated by a drastic increase in its Gini coefficient from .353 in 1970 to .499 in 1976. The positive change in the property Gini inequality and the increased share of property income had a significant adverse impact (+.0239 or 40.2%) on the overall HID. This would be based upon some important considerations:

1. Massive credit subsides to selected entrepreneurs. In an attempt to stimulate export-oriented industrialization, the government discriminately subsidized massive credits of financial resources by mobilizing public thrift saving, and monetary expansion to preferred industries and selected entrepreneurs at low interest rates, as shown in Table 56.

2. Low interest rate regime. In the 1970s, the government effectuated lower interest rates on bank deposits and loans than the existing high inflation rates. This resulted in the invisible wealth transfer from creditors (general public of thrift-savings) to debtors (government and subsidized entrepreneurs).

---

[65] The Bank of Korea, "Ownership of Listed Capital Stock," Monthly Economic Statistics, Vol. 27 (Jan. 1973), p. 59.

TABLE 56

FINANCIAL CREDIT SUBSIDIES BY BANKING SYSTEM, 1961-1979
(Unit: In current billion won)

| (1) Year | (2) Bank Notes (C) | (3) Reserve (R) | (4) Money Supply ($M_1$) | (5) Total Money Supply ($M_2$) | (6) Net Domestic Credits Financed by Banking System (NDC) | (7) Gross Investment (GI) |
|---|---|---|---|---|---|---|
| 1961 | 18 | 7 | --- | --- | --- | 39 |
| 1962 | 21 | 9 | 39 | 52 | 51 (15%) | 46 |
| 1963 | 22 | 6 | 42 | 55 | 63 (13%) | 91 |
| 1964 | 28 | 5 | 49 | 64 | 68 (10%) | 101 |
| 1965 | 35 | 13 | 66 | 97 | 94 (12%) | 121 |
| 1966 | 47 | 44 | 65 | 157 | 120 (12%) | 224 |
| 1967 | 68 | 43 | 123 | 254 | 206 (20%) | 281 |
| 1968 | 96 | 60 | 178 | 437 | 368 (22%) | 428 |
| 1969 | 130 | 91 | 252 | 705 | 568 (26%) | 621 |
| 1970 | 159 | 144 | 308 | 898 | 718 (27%) | 719 |
| 1971 | 187 | 103 | 358 | 1,085 | 941 (29%) | 831 |
| 1972 | 245 | 171 | 519 | 1,452 | 1,217 (30%) | 874 |
| 1973 | 354 | 268 | 730 | 1,981 | 1,539 (29%) | 1,341 |
| 1974 | 455 | 321 | 946 | 2,457 | 2,504 (34%) | 2,274 |
| 1975 | 561 | 503 | 1,182 | 3,150 | 3,285 (34%) | 2,882 |
| 1976 | 736 | 695 | 1,544 | 4,205 | 3,836 (29%) | 3,378 |
| 1977 | 1,034 | 1,033 | 2,173 | 5,874 | 4,548 (27%) | 4,665 |
| 1978 | 1,492 | 1,269 | 2,714 | 7,929 | --- | 7,138 |
| 1979 | 1,818 | 1,607 | 3,275 | 9,878 | --- | 10,597 |

SOURCE: The Bank of Korea, Economic Statistics Yearbook, Seoul, various years.

NOTE: Column (2): Cumulated signiorage and inflation tax (high power money) = C (currency in circulation held by non-bank public) + R (reserve).

Column (4): $M_1$ = C (currency in circulation) + D (demand deposit).

Column (5): $M_2$ = C + D + TD (time deposit).

Column (6): NDC = Gross domestic credit - time and savings deposits of corporation.

3. Revenue from seigniorage-cum-inflation tax.[66] Korea's government maintained inflationary financing by monetary expansion for development expenditures and subsidies to selected exporting entrepreneurs at preferential interest rates. In other words, the government collected the revenue from a seigniorage-cum-inflation tax[67] on the general public (workers and underprivileged entrepreneurs) and subsidized preferred exporting entrepreneurs at low interest rates. Thus, the substantial amounts of real financial resources were indirectly transferred from the general public, including unprivileged entrepreneurs, to the government and ultimately to selected entrepreneurs.

Consequently, in the case of the low interest policy in comparison with high inflation rates, the general public was discouraged from savings, and the privileged entrepreneurs' corporations improperly increased their ownership of capital stock in the 1970s.

As we have already seen, the overall distribution of income has a number of factor components which differ in type and in impact on overall inequality for the households' income. Before 1970, the

---

[66]New money creation (change in money stock each year) is just the same as revenue from imposing inflation tax on the real cash balances held by the general public. This is simply expressed as follows: $M/p = m\pi$, where $\dot{M}/p$, $m$, and $\pi$ are changes in real money stock, real cash balances held by the nonbank public, and inflation rates, respectively.

This implies that the government squeezes real financial resources from the general public by inflationary financing through monetary expansion. Thus, the stock of high-powered bank notes and coins equals the cumulated net government revenue from a seigniorage-cum-inflation tax. In more detailed information, see the following articles: Mundell, "Inflationary Finance"; Alvin L. Marty, "Growth, Satiety, and the Tax Revenue from Money Creation," Journal of Political Economy (September/October, 1973); and Ronald I. McKinnon, Money and Finance in Economic Growth and Development (New York: Marcel Dekker, 1976).

[67]The bank notes and coins (high-powered money) issued by the central bank (the Bank of Korea) increased at an annual rate of 30%, while the general price (CPI) increased at an annual rate of 19% during the period 1970-1979.

economic growth-relevant effects (the intersectoral reallocation effect and the functional distribution effect) had an adverse impact on the overall HID. The highly favorable factor Gini effect (-.0445 or -132.8%), however, overwhelmingly exceeded the two adverse effects so that the net effect resulted in the favorable change in the overall Gini $J_Y$ (-.0335) for the period 1965-1970.

Therefore, the intersectoral and intrasectoral economic growth patterns failed to improve the overall distribution of income in Korea. The favorable distribution of income, however, was caused mainly by the factor Gini effect which was related to the favorable distribution of human and financial capitals during this period.

After 1970, the overall distribution of income deteriorated much more than it improved before 1970. The causation of the unfavorable change in overall Gini (+.0595) could be traced to the three effects. The intersectoral reallocation effect (+.0008 or 1.3%) and the functional distribution effect (+.0009 or 1.5%) made things slightly worse, but the unfavorable factor Gini effect (+.0578 or 97.2%) mainly due to the unfavorable distribution of financial capital by the industrial development policy contributed to making things significantly worse in this period. Thus, the factor Gini effect became a major causation factor which determined the unfavorable distribution of income for overall households for the period 1970-1976 as shown on Table 54.

Generally, the overall distribution of income in Korea improved in the course of remarkable economic growth until 1970 and then significantly deteriorated after this date. Thus, it should be noted that the distribution pattern Korea experienced in its continuous economic growth was that of a U-shaped configuration rather than the inverse U-shaped pattern which usually took place in the LDCs.

Kuznets and Myrdal hypothesized that economic growth through the industrialization strategy in the developing countries leads to an adverse effect on the equality of income distribution in the early stage of development, and then turns better thereafter in the course of economic growth. Korea's distribution pattern was the opposite of the Kuznets-Myrdal hypothesis. Thus, Korea's experience indicates that there is nothing inevitable about the appearance of a Kuznets-Myrdal effect in the course of rapid economic growth.

Taiwan's economic growth pattern does not support the Kuznets-Myrdal hypothesis, either. During the past two decades, Taiwan's experience is that her economic growth and favorable distribution were consistent as twin objectives of development strategy in the development process. The sustained favorable changes in overall HID were mainly achievable through the basic forces underlying the pattern of growth.

Taiwan's overall distribution of income continually improved by a decline of its Gini inequality form .3208 in 1964 to .2928 in 1970, and further to .2887 in 1978 as shown in Table 57. This continuous improvement is attributable to the causative effects Taiwan experienced during the period 1964-1978.

TABLE 57

THE GINI COEFFICIENTS OF FACTOR INCOME COMPONENTS AND THEIR SHARES IN TAIWAN, 1964-1978

| Variable | Notation | 1964 | 1970 | 1978 |
|---|---|---|---|---|
| Overall Gini. . . . . . | $(J_Y)$ | .3208 | .2928 | .2887 |
| Wage Gini . . . . . . . | $(J_W)$ | .2365 | .2775 | .2789 |
| Property Gini . . . . . | $(J_R)$ | .4487 | .4278 | .3777 |
| Agricultural Gini . . . | $(J_A)$ | .3543 | .0655 | .0718 |
| Nonagricultural Gini. . | $(J_V)$ | .3123 | .3255 | .3077 |
| Wage Share. . . . . . . | $(s_W)$ | .4324 | .5454 | .6210 |
| Property Share. . . . . | $(s_R)$ | .2401 | .2558 | .2251 |
| Agricultural Share. . . | $(s_A)$ | .2754 | .1307 | .0729 |
| Nonagricultural Share . | $(s_V)$ | .6725 | .8012 | .8761 |

SOURCE: Adapted from Shirley W. Y. Kuo, et al., The Taiwan Success Story (1952-1979) (Boulder: Westview Press, 1981).

NOTE: The relative shares do not quite add up to 1 because the merged category of mixed incomes, which constitute less than 10% of the total, was neglected.

The growth-relevant effects (the intersectoral reallocation effect and functional distribution effect) succeeded in improving the overall distribution of income in Taiwan while these same effects failed in improving the overall HID in Korea. In the early development period, nonagricultural income was distributed more equally than agricultural income in Taiwan. Under this condition, the rise in the distributive share of the well-distributed nonagricultural income would serve to improve Taiwan's overall HID. As a result, the intersectoral reallocation effect (-.0061 or -8.0%) had a second dominant favorable impact on the overall HID before 1970 in Taiwan (see Table 58).

After 1970, Taiwan's agricultural income distribution deteriorated slightly by an increase in its Gini inequality from .0655 in 1970 to .0718 in 1978. In addition, the agricultural income switched from Type 1 income to Type 2 income after 1970. However, the share of the well-distributed agricultural income decreased relative to that of the poorly distributed nonagricultural income in the intersectoral resources reallocation process. This condition resulted in a positive effect (+.0087 or +147.5%) on the inequality of the overall distribution of income.

In the case of functional distribution, Taiwan's wage income was always distributed more equally than her property income during the entire period of 1964-1978 (see Table 57). To make matters better, the share of wage income relative to property income continued to increase through time due to the labor-using technological progress in the functional distribution of the industrial sector. These two conditions brought about the reduction of nonagricultural income inequality and thus had a favorable impact on the overall HID (-.0054 before 1970 and -.0034 after 1970) in both periods, as shown in Table 58.

With respect to Taiwan's factor Gini effect, the agricultural Gini effect (-.0795 or -104.2%) had the most dominant favorable impact on the overall equality of income before 1970. Thus, Taiwan's agricultural-oriented growth path enhanced an important role of agricultural income as a HID equalizer and contributed to the great improvement in the overall distribution of income in Taiwan.

After 1970, however, the nonagricultural Gini effect (-.0120 or -203.4%) had the greatest favorable impact on the overall distribution of income. Consequently, the industry-driven growth pattern after 1970 played a major role of nonagricultural income in improving the overall HID in Taiwan.

In sum, in the agriculture-oriented growth path before 1970, the growth-relevant effects (R and D effects) and the factor Gini effect were all shown as a favorable impact on the overall HID, and thus all the three favorable effects add up to -.0763 during the period 1964-1970, which contributed to a remarkable reduction in the overall income inequality in Taiwan.

After 1970, in the course of drastic changes in intersectoral economic activities in favor of the nonagricultural sector, the intersectoral reallocation effect (R) was unable to have any further favorable impact on the overall distribution of income. Thus, the reallocation effect was shown as an adverse impact (+.0087) on the

TABLE 58

EFFECTS OF REALLOCATION, FUNCTIONAL DISTRIBUTION, AND FACTOR GINI ON OVERALL DISTRIBUTION OF INCOME IN TAIWAN, 1964-1978

| Variable | Notation | Total Estimated Change | | Percentage Distribution of Estimated Change | |
|---|---|---|---|---|---|
| | | 1964-1970 | 1970-1978 | 1964-1970 (%) | 1970-1978 (%) |
| Overall Gini | $dJ_Y$ | -.0763 | -.0059 | 100.0 | 100.0 |
| Reallocation Effect | R | -.0061 | +.0087 | -8.0 | 147.5 |
| Functional Distribution Effect | D | -.0054 | -.0034 | -7.1 | -57.6 |
| Factor Gini Effect | B | -.0668 | -.0112 | -87.5 | -189.8 |
| Agricultural Gini | $J_AE$ | -.0795 | +.0008 | -104.2 | 13.6 |
| Nonagricultural Gini | $J_VE$ | +.0127 | -.0120 | 16.6 | -203.4 |
| Wage Gini | $J_WE$ | +.0177 | +.0008 | 23.2 | 13.6 |
| Property Gini | $J_RE$ | -.0050 | -.0128 | -6.6 | -216.9 |

SOURCE: Calculated according to the differential decomposition equation (Equation 34) on the base of data in Table 57.

NOTE: $dJ_Y = R + D + B$ and $B = J_AE + J_VE$, where $J_VE = J_WE + J_RE$.

overall HID. However, in the growth path of labor-intensive industrialization in the nonagricultural sector, the functional distribution effect still had a favorable impact (-.0034) on the overall HID, even though it was not strong enough to offset the unfavorable reallocation effect (+.0087). Consequently, the growth-relevant (net) effect was shown as an unfavorable impact (+.0053) on the overall distribution of income in Taiwan.

However, the factor Gini (B) had a strongly favorable effect on the overall HID. This favorable factor Gini effect (-.0112 or -189.8%) was strong enough to offset the growth-relevant adverse effect (+.0053), so that the overall net effect after 1970 was still shown as a favorable impact (-.0059) on the overall distribution of income. The overall favorable effect after 1970, however, was not as strong as that before 1970.

These quantitative analytical results imply that Taiwan's growth-development pattern affected a favorable distribution of income during the entire period. Thus, as shown in Table 59, Taiwan experienced a "straight downward pattern," in terms of Gini inequality, of improvement in the distribution of income in the course of rapid economic growth in the 1960s and the 1970s. In other words, Taiwan's developmental path managed to achieve a more equitable distribution from the benefits of economic growth; which is to say that it achieved "growth with equality" rather than "growth with inequality."

As has been shown, this sustained favorable distribution of income for the overall households was accompanied mainly through the basic forces underlying a natural path of growth, rather than the

TABLE 59

THE EFFECTS OF REALLOCATION, FUNCTIONAL DISTRIBUTION, AND FACTOR GINI ON THE OVERALL HID

| Country | Variable | Period | | Overall Distribution Pattern* |
|---|---|---|---|---|
| | | (1965-1970) | (1970-1976) | |
| Korea | Total Net Effect | - | + | U shaped |
| | Reallocation Effect | + | + | |
| | Functional d. Effect | + | + | |
| | Factor Gini Effect | - | + | |
| | | (1964-1970) | (1970-1978) | |
| Taiwan | Total Net Effect | - | - | shaped (Straight downward) |
| | Reallocation Effect | - | + | |
| | Functional d. Effect | - | - | |
| | Factor Gini Effect | - | - | |

SOURCE: Tables 54 and 58

NOTE: +: unfavorable effect on onverall HID. -: favorable effect on overall HID.

*The overall distribution pattern describes the relationship between the overall inequality (Gini coefficient) and the economic growth (GNP per capita).

directly coercive redistribution by means of artificial taxation and transfer system. Thus, Taiwan chose the most efficient and natural method of tackling the maldistribution of income that takes place in the drastic industrialization strategy in the LDCs.

# CHAPTER VI

## SUMMARY AND CONCLUSIONS

Distribution is the result of economic growth. Thus, this distribution is to be analyzed in terms of a country's particular development policy and growth patterns in order to perceive the causal relationship between growth and distribution. Accordingly, this study has attempted to trace Korea's particular experience to the relation between growth and distribution by investigating the effect of development policy and growth patterns on changes in the overall distribution of income.

In an attempt to achieve a "big-push" in industrialization, Korea's government continually subsidized massive credits of financial resources to the preferred industrial sector by inducing foreign borrowings, mobilizing domestic savings, and even inflationary financing at low interest rates. Such a development policy brought about an immoderate increase in capital in the nonagricultural sector, thus leaving the agricultural sector lagging from the begining of development (an intersectoral unbalanced growth path).

According to conventional development theory, the role of the agricultural sector is very important to fuel the expansion of the industrial sector. The agricultural sector's function is to serve as an essential source of food, manpower, agricultural surplus capital for industrial wage funds, and raw materials for industrial usage.

In the meantime, the industrial capital growth must be harmonized with agricultural development in a fine-tuned fashion so that the improved agricultural productivity leads to food-price stability and the subsequent stabilization of industrial terms of trade in the development process. These stable terms of trade will continually curb wage inflation and will simultaneously stimulate labor absorption in the nonagricultural sector (an intersectoral balanced growth path).

Taiwan's economy followed this type of intersectorally balanced growth path. Korea's experience, however, provides little evidence for this conventional theory. On the contrary, Korea's economy illustrates a process of immoderate capital-intesive industrialization in the context of an open economy from the beginning, thus leaving its agricultural sector neglected from the outset and requiring the importation of food and raw materials early in the growth path. Consequently, the intersectorally unbalanced growth path in Korea had a considerable effect, not only on the sectoral distribution, but also on the functional distribution and the overall size distribution of income.

In the course of industrial development, the economic resouces have been substantially reallocated from the agricultural sector to the nonagricultural sector, transferring a large portion of the labor force, withdrawing the cultivated land from the agricultural sector for urban-industrial usage, and subsidizing massive financial capital (general public savings, foreign savings, and monetary expansion) to the industrial sector.

In this reallocation of resources, which did not favor the agricultural sector, the only way to increase agricultural output was to improve agricultural productivity (the nonphysical economic factor). However, Korea's agricultural economy experienced relatively slow growth in productivity during this period.

To make matters worse, some unfavorable agricultural policies--continuous food importation, the low grain price policy, and the fixed land tenure system--definitely led to a lack of incentive for the farmer to not only increase agricultural production, but also to enhance agricultural modernization.

As a result of inadequate agricultural participation, the agricultural economy had to face such serious problems as a decreasing food self-sufficiency and a widening income gap between the rural and urban sectors before 1970.

However, the government launched the New Community Movement (Saemaul Undong) in order to make a rural effort, maintaining the high grain price policy (the two-price system) with the government subsidies financed through monetary expansion during the period of 1970-1975. This resulted in the favorable agricultural terms of trade (see Table 22) and the favorable distribution of rural households' income between the two sectors (see Table 23). The share of agricultural income in the national income declined less than it would have without the high grain-price policy.

However, this grain deficit management had a negative effect on the stability of price level, so far as it was deficit-financed by monetary expansion. Thus, the high grain-price policy returned to the low grain-price policy after 1975.

This grain-price policy caused a relatively greater decline in agriculture's share of national income from 37.9% in 1961 to 24.3% in 1970 (an annual growth rate of -5%). From 1970 to 1975, however, a relatively smaller decline occurred, resulting in a decrease from 24.3% in 1970 to 23.5% in 1975 (an annual growth rate of -.7%). Next, the downward trend again increased to a degree with a decline of -6.2% annual growth rate, as witnessed by the decrease from 23.5% in 1975 to 18.2% in 1979.

Meanwhile, in the course of industrial expansion, the government mobilized general public savings, foreign borrowings, and even inflationary financing by monetary expansion, and then subsidized those massive credits of financial resources to the preferred industrial sector at a preferential interest rate which was much lower than the existing rate of inflation.

Consequently, this financial policy for industrialization led to a high increase in entrepreneurs' profit due to the high rate of return on capital, the low preferential interest rate, and the existing high rate of inflation. In this situation, profit-maximizing entrepreneurs were further induced to substitute capital for labor after the economic turning point (around 1966) where the unlimited supply of labor became exhausted and industrial wage began to increase.

From the theoretical point of view at this point (see Chapter II), capital and wage level became so closely dependent on each other that every increase in capital directly fed a corresponding increase in wage. In turn, every increase in wage level immediately fueled an additional increase in capital. Such a spiral acceleration was generated, whereby Korea's industrial capital stock has been dramatically and improperly increased at an annual rate of 11.4% during the past two decades.

This immoderately increased capital did not play a major role in the contribution to an increase in nonagricultural income, but labor input growth (7.2% per year) played a more important role in the total income growth than did any other factors (see Table 29, row 7). Thus, the improperly increased capital was inefficiently utilized in the production process, as compared to labor utilization. Accordingly, the nonagricultural economy experienced low growth in productivity, due to the inefficient combinations of factor inputs. This, in turn, did lead to a reduction in potential national income.

In addition to the spiral wage-inflation effect due to the drastic increase in industrial capital, the poor agricultural development in Korea led to a relatively earlier advent of economic turning point. Thus, Korea's economy was forced to raise industrial real wages relatively earlier and faster than usual. The wage-inflation factor, due to the unbalanced growth path, immediately brought about a drastic increase in the factor price level after the economic turning point (around 1966: see Table 38, column 2, Figure 2, and Table 32, column 6).

Furthermore, the unbalanced growth path which caused a high growth in factor price was also accompanied by a relatively lower growth in total productivity (2.9%) in the nonagricultural sector. Thus, the low productivity improvement could not absorb a relatively high growth in factor price enough to alleviate wage-push inflationary pressure. Consequently, Korea's economy experienced high rates of inflation and inflationary economic growth (see Chapter III and Table 32, column 6).

On the other hand, Taiwan's economy, which was based upon the balanced growth path, experienced a low growth in factor price (10.0% per year) and a relatively high growth in productivity (3.1%). Accordingly, the difference (6.9% annual growth rate of general price level) between the two growths became much smaller than that of Korea's unbalanced growth path. Therefore, Taiwan enjoyed economic prosperity, along with price stability during the development period (see Table 34).

In the analysis of functional distribution in Korea's nonagricultural sector, the labor share diminished in the course of the technical substitution of capital and labor by relative changes in factor prices, due to the market forces. More technically, the capital-intesive industrialization experienced sustained labor-saving technological progress, both in the 1960s and in the 1970s, except for the subperiod of 1965-1970. However, the strength of labor saving progress has been higher in the 1970s than in the 1960s (see Table 36).

Taiwan's nonagricultural economy was exactly the opposite

of Korea's. The labor-intensive industrialization achieved labor-using technolgoical progress. That is, a steady improvement in the labor share during the last two decades in Taiwan's nonagricultural sector (Table 44). Those growth-relevant distributions (inter-sectoral and intrasectoral) in both countries definitely affected their overall size-distribution of income, respectively.

According to the analytical results of Korea and of Taiwan, it should be noted that the rapid economic growth in the LDCs can be accompanied by improved income distribution as in Korea and Taiwan in the 1960s. That is, the twin goals of "Growth and Equality" can be achieved at the same time in the early stage of development, rather than being mutually exclusive as in the Kuznets-Myrdal hypothesis.

In the 1960s, the empirical studies of Korea and Taiwan suggested a definite rejection of the pessimistic hypothesis of trade-off between growth and equality in the early stage of development. These two countries have achieved very impressive rates of growth in national income (9.8% in Korea and 9.7% in Taiwan), exports (35% in Korea and 28% in Taiwan), and employment. At the same time, both countries also achieved a great improvement in the overall household distribution of income.

Korea, however, deviated from the path of growth with equality and, thus, experienced a worsening of the distribution of income along with considerable rates of inflation after 1970. In the meantime, Taiwan has continued to keep track of growth with equality and has managed to avoid both economic evils in the 1970s.

Therefore, Korea experienced a particular distribution pattern, namely a "U-shaped" pattern of the distribution of income, while Taiwan's experience indicates a "straight downward" pattern of improvement in the overall HID as in Table 59.

Here arises an important question about how Taiwan's economy managed to reconcile growth to distribution and why Korea's economy could not achieve the same performance. This fundamental question involves the underlying preconditions for the distribution of income and the differences of the original growth pattern between the two countries as has been seen from analyzing the interplay of economic growth and income distribution.

The economic preconditions for an improved distribution of income were considerably more favorable in Taiwan than in Korea. In the early period of development (the 1950s and the early 1960s), Taiwan's economy was oriented from the better preparation of agricultural development via its productivity improvement (see Table 15). This agriculture-oriented growth pattern led to the economic condition under which agricultural income was distributed less equally than nonagricultural income (agricultural income was Type 1 income, and nonagricultural income, Type 2 income).

Meanwhile, the relatively balanced growth in the nonagricultual sector, which was geared to the agricultural modernization in a fine-tuned fashion, brought about the condition that wage income was distributed more equally than property income (wage income was Type 2 income, and property income, Type 1 income).

Under these economic preconditions, the rise in the distributive share of well-distributed nonagricultural income relative to that of maldistributed agricultural income in the course of the intersectoral economic growth, served to improve the overall distribution of income in Taiwan (the intersectoral reallocation effect).

In addition to the growth path of labor-intensive industrialization in the nonagricultural sector, the rise in the share of the well-distributed wage income relative to that of property income also served to improve the overall HID throughout the entire period in Taiwan (the functional distribution effect).

Furthermore, the drastic improvement in agricultural income equality in the course of industrial growth enhanced an important role of agricultural income as an income distribution equalizer and contributed to the great improvement in the overall HID before 1970 (Gini factor effect).

After 1970, as the economic center of gravity shifted from agricultural to nonagricultural activities, the agricultural income switched from Type 1 income to Type 2 income due to the remarkable improvement in agricultural income equality (see agricultural Gini in Table 57). Accordingly, the rise in the distributive share of maldistributed nonagricultural income (Type 1 income) caused a slight increase in the inequality of HID.

However, the growth path of labor-intensive industrialization in the nonagricultural sector still had a strongly favorable effect on both functional distribution and factor Gini which, in turn, reduced the overall inequality of income as a whole. Therefore, Taiwan's balanced growth path resulted in a "straight downward" pattern of improvement in the distribution of income, as well as a stability of price level in Taiwan.

However, Korea's economic preconditions and growth patterns were exactly the opposite of Taiwan's in the same period. The economic preconditions were unfavorable to the economic growth pattern in Korea.

From the beginning of development, Korea's government strategically built up the strength of capital-intensive industrialization, leaving the agricultural sector lagging, as mentioned earlier. This unbalanced growth path not only caused inflationary economic growth, but also a worsening of the overall distribution of income after 1970.

In the early period of development (the early 1960s), Korea's economy was oriented toward a strategic industrial development via a drastic capital-deepening growth path in the industrial sector in the face of inadequate agricultural participation (see Chapter II and III). This industry-oriented growth pattern led to the economic condition under which nonagricultural income was distributed less equally than agricultural income in Korea (nonagricultural income was Type 1 income and agricultural income was Type 2 income). Here, the rise in the distributive share of maldistributed nonagricultural income in the course of the economic concentration toward the nonagricultural sector obviously deteriorated the overall distribution of income throughout the entire period in Korea (the intersectoral reallocation effect).

In the unbalanced growth path, Korea's precondition of

intrasectoral income inequality in the nonagricultural sector was that of wage income being distributed less equally than property income before 1970. The wage income, however, switched from Type 1 income to Type 2 income after 1970. In this relation, the rise in the relative share of wage income (Type 1 income), due to the labor-using technological progress in the subperiod of 1965-1970 (see Table 36) resulted in a worsening of the overall distribution of income before 1970 (functional distribution effect).

After 1970, the rise in the functional share of maldistributed property income (Type 1 income), due to the capital-using technological progress, also brought about the unfavorable distribution of income as a whole. Thus, Korea's growth-relevant factors (intersectoral reallocation effect and functional distribution effect) failed to improve the overall distribution of income in both periods in Korea.

Fortunately, the equality of the increased nonagricultural income remarkably improved, due to the drastic reduction in wage Gini and property Gini coefficients before 1970. This favorable nonagricultural factor Gini effect was strong enough to offset not only the unfavorable agricultural factor Gini effect, but also the growth-relevant adverse effects, so that the overall net effect before 1970 was seen as a favorable impact on the overall distribution of income in Korea.

After 1970, however, the most unfavorable Gini effect--mainly due to the distribution of distorted financial capital by the industrial development policy--caused a significant worsening of the overall distribution of income along with the growth-relevant adverse effects.

In conclusion, Taiwan's economy experienced an "agriculture-oriented economic growth," along with a labor-using technological progress in the industrial sector, such as a balanced economic growth path. In doing so, Taiwan achieved not only a considerable price stability, but also a more equitable income distribution from the benefit of economic growth. Thus, Taiwan enjoyed economic prosperity, along with economic stability and equitable distribution of income during the entire period.

In the same period, Korea's economy followed an "industry-oriented economic growth" with capital-biased technological progress due to the improper capital growth in the nonagricultural sector, such as unbalanced growth path. This inevitably led to a considerable inflationary growth and a significant worsening of the overall distribution of income after 1970.

Finally, there is a considerable volume of literature in relation to the effect of Korea's distorted financial system on the distribution of income during this study period. It is suggested that the distorted financial system for industrialization be examined in terms of redistribution of income. It is regretted that this paper could not be expanded to include the effects of the distorted financial system on the distribution of income. It is currently being considered and may be presented in a future work.

## SELECTED BIBLIOGRAPHY


Adelman, Irma, and Robinson, Sherman. Income Distribution Policy in Developing Countries (A Case Study of Korea). Stanford: Stanford University Press, 1978.

Aitchison, John, and Brown, J. A. C. The Lognormal Distribution. Cambridge: Cambridge University Press, 1969.

Arrow, Kenneth J.; Chenery, Hollis B.; Minhas, B. S.; and Solow, Robert M. "Capital-Labor Substitution and Economic Efficiency." The Review of Economics and Statistics, Vol. XLIII. August 1961.

Ban, Sung Hwan; Moon, Pal Young; and Perkins, Dwight H. Rural Development (1965-1976). Cambridge: Harvard University Press, 1980.

Bailey, Martin J. "The Welfare Cost of Inflationary Finance." Journal of Political Economy, April 1956.

The Bank of Korea. Economic Statistics Yearbook. Seoul: 1977.

The Bank of Korea. Monthly Economic Statistics. Seoul: January 1965 to January 1981.

Boulding, Kenneth E., and Wilson, Thomas F., ed. Redistribution Through the Financial System. New York: Praeger Special Studies, 1978.

Bronfenbrenner, Martin. Income Distribution Theory. Chicago: Aldine Publishing Co., 1976.

Brown, Murray. On the Theory and Measurement of Technological Change. Cambridge: Cambridge University Press, 1966.

Brown, Murray, ed. The Theory and Empirical Analysis of Production. New York: Columbia University Press, 1967.

Brown, Murray, and de Cani, John S. "Technological Change and Distribution of Income." International Economic Review, Vol. 4, September 1963.

Budd, Edward C. "Postwar Change in the Size Distribution of Income in the U.S." American Economic Review, May 1970.

Budd, Edward C., and Sieders, David F. "The Impact of Inflation on the Distribution of Income and Wealth." American Economic Review, Vol. 61, May 1971.

Chenery, Hollis B., ed. Redistribution With Growth. London: Oxford University Press, 1974.

Chenery, Hollis B., and Syrquin, Moises. Patterns of Development (1950-1970). London: Oxford University Press, 1975.

Choo, Hak-Chung, and Kim, Dae-Mo. Probable Size Distribution of Income in Korea. Seoul: KDI, 1978.

Cole, David C., and Park, Yung Chul. Financial Development in Korea (1945-1978). Cambridge: Harvard University Press, 1983.

Craven, John. The Distribution of the Product. London: George Allen Urwin, 1978.

Domar, E. D. Essays in the Theory of Economic Growth. New York: Oxford University Press, 1957.

Fei, John C. H., and Ranis, Gustav. Development of the Labor Surplus Economy. New Haven: The Economic Center, Yale University Press, 1964.

________. "Development and Employment in the Open Dualistic Economy." American Economic Review, October 1979.

Fei, John C. H.; Ranis, Gustav; and Kuo, Shirley W. Y. Growth with Equity: Taiwan Case. New York: Oxford University Press, 1979.

Ferguson, C. E. "Substitution, Technical Progress and Returns to Scale." American Economic Review, Vol. 55, May 1965.

________. "Time-Series Production Functions, and Technological Progress in American Manufacturing Industry." Journal of Political Economy, Vol. 73, April 1965.

Floystad, Gunnar. "A Note on Estimating the Elasticity of Substitution between Labour and Capital from Norwegian Time Series Data." Swedish Journal of Economics, Vol. 75, March 1973.

Frankel, Marvin. "The Production Function in Allocation and Growth: Analysis." American Economic Review, Vol. LII, December 1962.

Galenson, Walter, ed. Economic Growth and Structural Change in Taiwan. Ithaca, N.J.: Cornell University Press, 1979.

Han, K. C. Estimates of Korean Capital and Inventory Coefficients in 1968. Seoul: Yonsei University, 1970.

Hapdong News Agency. Korean Annual. Seoul: 1965-1979.

Hicks, John Richard. The Theory of Wage. London: McMillan and Col, 1935.

________. Capital and Growth. London: Oxford University Press, 1965.

Ho, Yhi-Min. Agricultural Development of Taiwan (1903-1960). Kingsport: Vanderbilt University Press, 1966.

Hong, Won-Tak. Factor Supply and Factor Intensity of Trade in Korea. Seoul: KDI, 1976.

Hong, W. T., and Krueger, A. O., ed. Trade and Development in Korea. Seoul: KDI, 1975.

Jeong, D. K. "A Study on Impact of Economic Growth on Rural-Urban Income Distribution in Korea." Korean Journal, September 1984.

Kendrick, John W. Postwar Productivity Trends in the U.S. (1948-1969). New York: NBER, 1973.

________. Productivity Trends in the U.S. Princeton: Princeton University Press, 1961.

Kendrick, John W., and Sato, Ryuzo. "Factor Prices, Productivity, and Economic Growth." American Economic Review, December 1963.

Kendrick, John W., and Vaccara, Beatrice N., ed. New Development in Productivity Measurement and Analysis. Chicago: Chicago University Press, 1980.

Kim, Kwang Suk, and Roemer, Michael. Growth and Structural Transformation. Chambridge: Harvard University Press, 1979.

Kravis, Irving B. "Relative Income Shares in Fact and Theory." American Economic Review, Vol. 49, December 1959.

Krueger, Anne O. The Development Role of the Foreign Sector and Aid. Cambridge: Harvard University Press, 1979.

Kuo, Shirley W. Y. The Taiwan Economy in Transition. Boulder: Westview Press, 1983.

Kuo, Shirley W. Y.; Ranis, Gustav; and Fei, John C. H. The Taiwan Success Story: Rapid Growth with Improved Distribution in the Republic of China (1952-1979). Boulder: Westview Press, 1981.

Kuznets, Paul W. Economic Growth and Structure in the Republic of Korea. New Haven: Yale University Press, 1977.

Kuznets, Simon. Population, Capital and Growth. New York: W. W. Norton & Co., Inc., 1973.

________. Growth, Population, and Income Distribution (Selected Essay). New York: Norton & Co., Inc., 1979.

Lewis, William A. "Economic Development with Unlimited Surplus Labour." The Manchest School XXII, 1954, pp. 139-191.

Liu, T'ai-Ying. Report on Factors Which Hinder or Help Productivity Improvement in the Republic of China. Tokyo: Asian Productivity Organization, 1980.

Marty, Alvin L. "Growth, Satiety, and the Tax Revenue from Money Creation." Journal of Political Economy, September 1973.

McKinnon, Ronald I. "Wage, Capital Costs, and Employment in Manufacturing." Econometrica, Vol. 30, July 1962.

________, ed. "Wage, Capital Costs, and Employment in Manufacturing." Econometrica, Vol. 30, July 1962.

Meier, Gerald M. Leading Issues in Development Economics. New York: Oxford University Press, 1964.

Mizoguchi, Toshiyki; Kim, Do Hyung; and Chung, Young Il. "Overtime Changes of the Size Distribution of Household Income in Korea (1963-1971)." The Developing Economics, Vol. XIV, September 1976.

Mukerji, V. "A Generalized S.M.A.C. Function with Constant Ratios of Elasticity of Substitution." Review of Economic Studies, Vol. 30, October 1963.

Mundell, Robert. "Growth, Stability and Inflationary Finance." Journal of Political Economy, April 1965, pp. 97-109.

National Agricultural Cooperative Federation. Agricultural Cooperative Yearbook. Seoul: Ministry of Agricultural and Forestry, various years.

Nugent, Jeffrey B., and Walther, Robin J. "Short-run Changes in Rural Income Inequality; A Decomposition Analysis," Journal of Development Studies, Vol. 18, January 1982.

Pasinetti, Luigi L. "Rate of Profit and Income Distribution in Relation to the Rate of Economic Growth." Reivew of Economic Studies, Vol. 29, October 1962.

Phelps, Edmund S. "Substitution, Fixed Proportions, Growth, and Distribution." International Economic Review, Vol. 4, September 1963.

Paukert, F.; Skolka, J.; and Maton, J. Income Distribution Structure of Economy and Employment. London: International Labor Organization, 1981.

Sato, Ryuzo. "The Estimation of Biased Technological Progress and the Production Function." International Economic Review, January 1970.

Solow, Robert M. "Technical Change and the Aggregate Production Function." Review of Economic Statistics, August 1957.

________. "Substitution and Fixed Proportions in the Theory of Capital." Review of Economic Statistics, Vol. 29, June 1962.

________. "Technical Progress, Capital Formation and Economic Growth." American Economic Review, May 1962.

Wu, Chia-Sheng. "Productivity and Wage Structure in Taiwan's Manufacturing Sector (1966-1979)." Ph.D. dissertation, University of Utah, 1981.

For Product Safety Concerns and Information please contact our EU
representative GPSR@taylorandfrancis.com Taylor & Francis Verlag GmbH,
Kaufingerstraße 24, 80331 München, Germany

Printed and bound by CPI Group (UK) Ltd, Croydon, CR0 4YY
08/05/2025
01864370-0015